Heather Leyshon. 1994.

Heather Leyshon. 1994.

# HOW *WOULD* YOU SURVIVE AS AN ANCIENT
# EGYPTIAN?

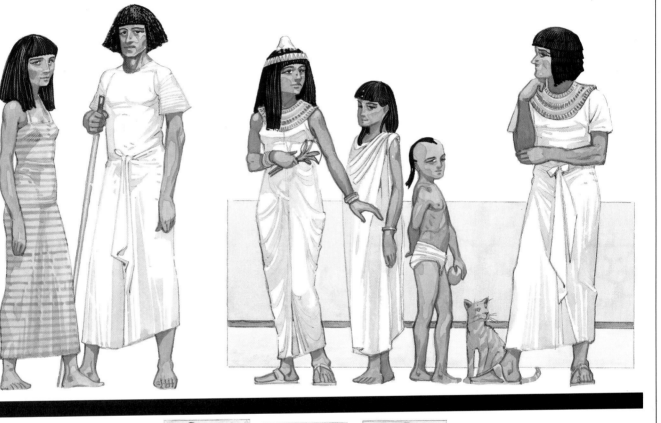

*Written by*
## Jacqueline Morley

*Illustrated by*
## John James

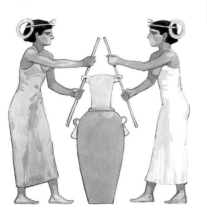

*Created & Designed by*
## David Salariya

## WATTS BOOKS

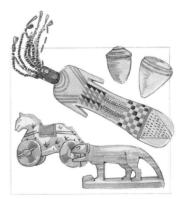

# LONDON • NEW YORK • SYDNEY

David Salariya     *Director*
Diana Holubowicz     *Editor*
Dr. Rosalie David     *Consultant*

## JACQUELINE MORLEY

is a graduate of Somerville College, Oxford. She has taught English and History, and now works as a freelance translator and writer. She has written historical fiction and non-fiction for children, and has a particular interest in the history of everyday life. She has also written **Entertainment** and **Clothes** in the *Timelines* series, **An Egyptian Pyramid** in the *Inside Story* series, and **How** *would* **you survive as a Viking?**

## JOHN JAMES

studied illustration at Eastbourne College of Art. Since leaving art school in 1983, he has specialised in historical reconstructions and architectural cross-sections. He is a major contributor to the *Timelines* and *X-Ray Picture Book* series. John James lives in East Sussex with his wife and daughters.

## DAVID SALARIYA

was born in Dundee, Scotland, where he studied illustration and printmaking. He has illustrated a wide range of books on botanical, historical and mythical subjects. He has created and designed many new series of books for publishers in the UK and overseas. In 1989 he established The Salariya Book Company. He lives in Brighton with his wife, the illustrator Shirley Willis.

Printed in Belgium

A CIP catalogue record for this book is available from the British Library.

First published in 1993 by WATTS BOOKS

## DR. ROSALIE DAVID

is an Egyptologist at Manchester Museum, and Director of the Manchester Egyptian Mummy Research Project and the Kahun Project. She has been consultant to the BBC television series *Chronicle* on several films about Egypt. Dr. David also acted as consultant on the *Inside Story* **An Egyptian Pyramid** which won the TES award in 1992.

WATTS BOOKS
96 Leonard Street
London EC2A 4RH
ISBN 0-7496–1089-1
Dewey Decimal Classification Number 932

# CONTENTS

BECOMING AN ANCIENT EGYPTIAN...

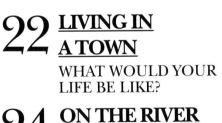
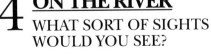

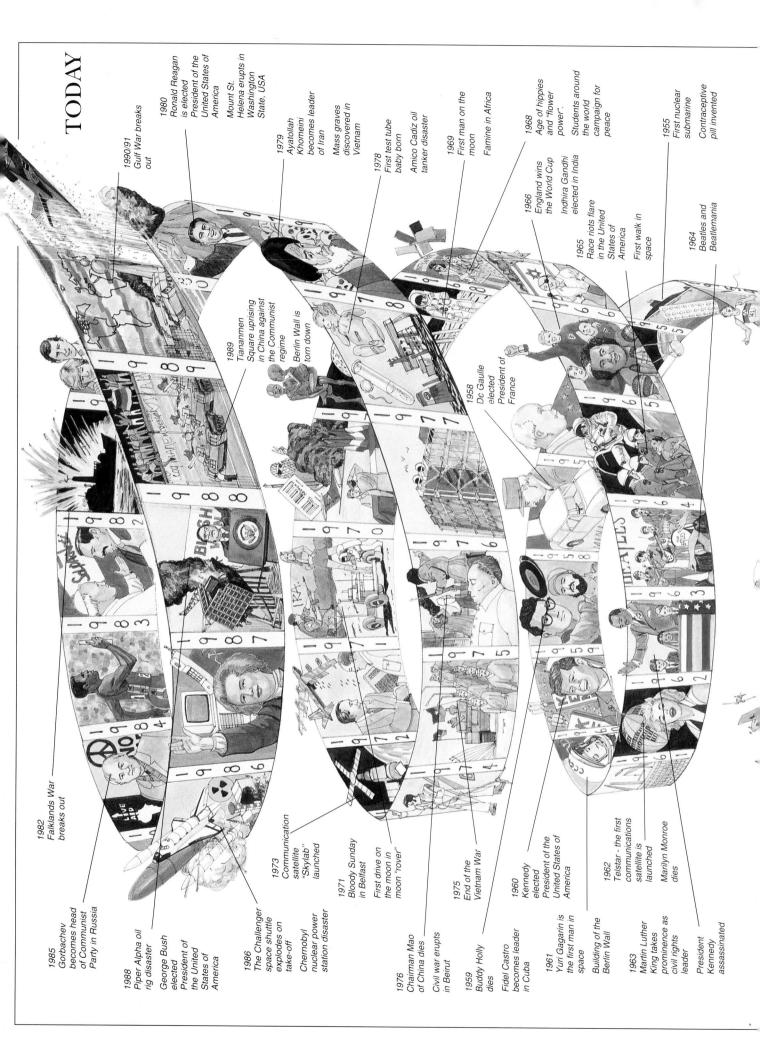

TODAY

1990/91
Gulf War breaks
out

1980
Ronald Reagan
is elected
President of the
United States of
America

Mount St.
Helena erupts in
Washington
State, USA

1979
Ayatollah
Khomeini
becomes leader
of Iran

Mass graves
discovered in
Vietnam

1978
First test tube
baby born

Amico Cadiz oil
tanker disaster

1969
First man on the
moon

Famine in Africa

1968
Age of hippies
and "flower
power".

Students around
the world
campaign for
peace

1966
England wins
the World Cup

Indhira Gandhi
elected in India

1965
Race riots flare
in the United
States of
America

First walk in
space

1955
First nuclear
submarine

Contraceptive
pill invented

1964
Beatles and
Beatlemania

1989
Tiananmen
Square uprising
in China against
the Communist
regime

Berlin Wall is
torn down

1958
De Gaulle
elected
President of
France

1985
Gorbachev
becomes head
of Communist
Party in Russia

1988
Piper Alpha oil
rig disaster

George Bush
elected
President of
the United
States of
America

1986
The Challenger
space shuttle
explodes on
take-off

Chernobyl
nuclear power
station disaster

1982
Falklands War
breaks out

1973
Communication
satellite
"Skylab"
launched

1971
Bloody Sunday
in Belfast

First drive on
the moon in
moon "rover"

1975
End of the
Vietnam War

1960
Kennedy
elected
President of the
United States of
America

1962
Telstar - the first
communications
satellite is
launched

Marilyn Monroe
dies

1976
Chairman Mao
of China dies

Civil war erupts
in Beirut

1959
Buddy Holly
dies

Fidel Castro
becomes leader
in Cuba

1961
Yuri Gagarin is
the first man in
space

Building of the
Berlin Wall

1963
Martin Luther
King takes
prominence as
civil rights
leader

President
Kennedy
assassinated

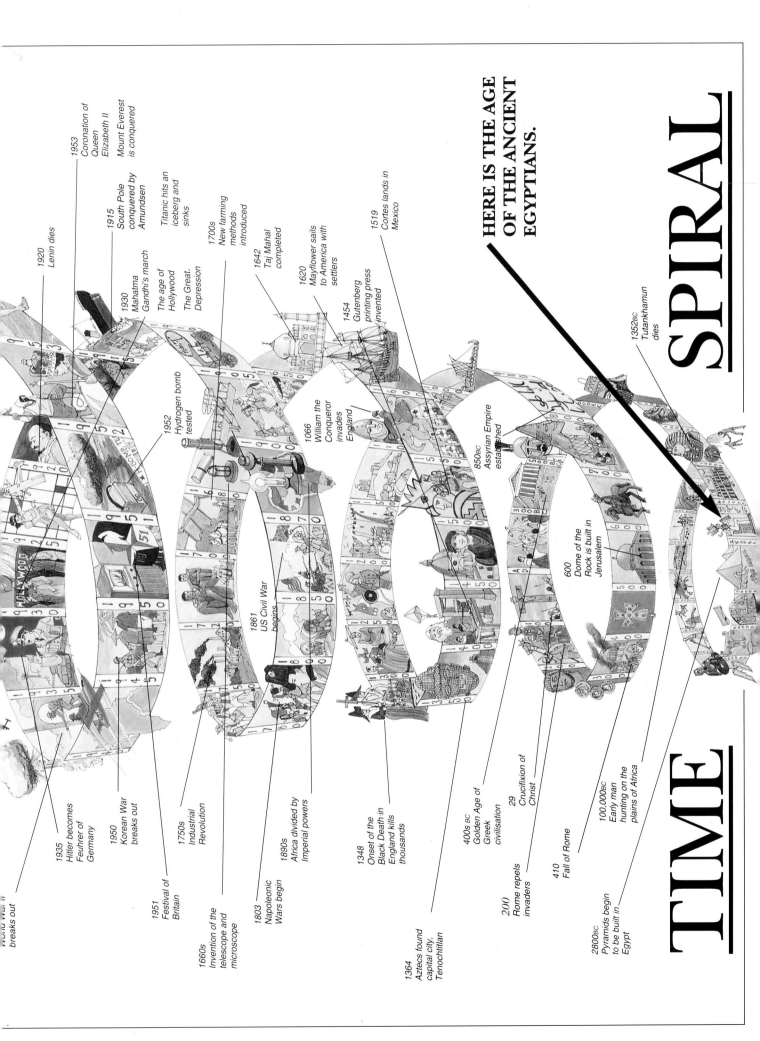

# SPIRAL

# TIME

HERE IS THE AGE
OF THE ANCIENT
EGYPTIANS.

World War II
breaks out

1935
Hitler becomes
Feuhrer of
Germany

1950
Korean War
breaks out

1951
Festival of
Britain

1660s
Invention of the
telescope and
microscope

1803
Napoleonic
Wars begin

1890s
Africa divided by
Imperial powers

1348
Onset of the
Black Death in
England kills
thousands

1364
Aztecs found
capital city,
Tenochtitlan

400s BC
Golden Age of
Greek
civilisation

200
Rome repels
invaders

29
Crucifixion of
Christ

410
Fall of Rome

100,000BC
Early man
hunting on the
plains of Africa

2800BC
Pyramids begin
to be built in
Egypt

1920
Lenin dies

1953
Coronation of
Queen
Elizabeth II

Mount Everest
is conquered

1915
South Pole
conquered by
Amundsen

Titanic hits an
iceberg and
sinks

1930
Mahatma
Gandhi's march

The age of
Hollywood

The Great
Depression

1700s
New farming
methods
introduced

1642
Taj Mahal
completed

1620
Mayflower sails
to America with
settlers

1454
Gutenberg
printing press
invented

1519
Cortes lands in
Mexico

1952
Hydrogen bomb
tested

1066
William the
Conqueror
invades
England

1861
US Civil War
begins

850BC
Assyrian Empire
established

600
Dome of the
Rock is built in
Jerusalem

1352BC
Tutankhamun
dies

## Time Stands Still

YOU ARE VISITING a land which never seems to change. For although ancient Egyptian history spans thirty centuries, during which pharaohs made war and built great tombs and temples, the lives of ordinary people hardly changed at all. They used the same tools, farmed in the same way, wore similar clothes and had the same beliefs. They thought their way was the right way, and saw no reason for change.

## Egyptian Landscape

LET US SUPPOSE that your time journey has brought you to Egypt during the New Kingdom (you can find out what that means on page 44) – in about 1450 BC. You will find yourself in a hot parched land. People have to rely on the Nile for water. Beyond the fertile land that the river waters, the desert stretches on either side. In the spring hot winds blow from it, bringing blistering sandstorms. The desert is an enemy, the home of demons.

## Water is Life

THE RIVER gives freshness and life, not only to humans but to a multitude of wild creatures. Its waters are full of fish, many of which are delicious to eat, like the grey mullet and Nile perch. The papyrus reeds of the delta and other marshy stretches teem with bird life – ducks, teal, crane, quail and ibis. Wild cats stalk prey there; mongoose hunt for eggs. Hippopotamuses wallow in the marshy pools and crocodiles glide silently by.

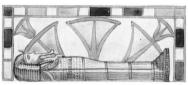

## Rich & Poor

IF YOU FIND yourself in a rich family you can look forward to a pleasant life, with servants to wait on you and time to enjoy yourself. But there were far more poor families than rich ones in ancient Egypt. If you grow up in one of these you will have to work hard with little hope of doing better in the future. People did not think this was unjust. They accepted that some people were born to work, and others to tell them what to do.

## The Pharaoh

THE KINGS of ancient Egypt were given the title of 'pharaoh' which means 'great house'. The pharaohs were very great indeed, for the Egyptians believed each one was a living god. The pharaoh used local governors and huge numbers of officials to carry out his orders. You will discover on your travels that people believe that it is the influence of their pharaoh that ensures that the river will flood each year.

## Dangers & Death

YOU MIGHT expect people to fear crocodiles and diseases, but the ancient Egyptians dreaded evil spirits far more. They believed that most misfortunes were caused by them. Childbirth was dangerous for mothers and babies alike, many of whom died. This accounts for the early average age of death – probably around 36. Many people lived much longer. The pharaoh, Pepi II, ruled for 94 years, the longest reign we know of in history.

## Wildlife & Plants

THE DESERT IS the home of lions, jackals, antelope, gazelle and ibex. Very little grows in the desert apart from thorn trees. In contrast the valley is green with growing crops and shade-giving trees. The most common trees are the date palm, the dom-palm, which has a nut-like fruit, and the sycamore fig. There are blossoming acacias and feathery tamarisk trees. The lotus, a Nile water lily, is a favourite flower.

## Taming the Nile

EVERYTHING the farmers grow depends on the waters of the Nile for life. Dykes prevent the flood from draining away and canals take it to the farmers' fields. Everyone has to co-operate. If careless landowners let their canals leak they rob other people of water. One of the most important departments of the king's government looks after the sharing of water along over one hundred kilometres of river.

## Towns & Villages

THERE ARE isolated villages in the western hills, built for workers who make the royal tombs, but most people live by the river. Villages are perched on land that the flood water does not cover. On the east bank you will see large cities, but not on the west. That is where the dead are buried. The ancient Egyptians believed that the dead travelled into the west, like the sun, and, like the sun, they would wake to a new life.

## Egyptian Gods

THE GODS played a large part in the lives of the ancient Egyptians. It was very important to keep the goodwill of the gods, for without their help disasters might happen to Egypt. The gods liked great festivals in their honour, which the people also enjoyed. The gods also liked to be given huge temples, and the pharaohs liked to build them, for in this way they created monuments to be remembered by.

## Neighbours

IF YOU WERE a wealthy ancient Egyptian you would probably travel quite a lot. Travel meant travel within Egypt. The ancient Egyptians were not at all interested in seeing how foreigners lived, or travelling to their lands. They thought that people beyond their borders were very unfortunate to live in lands so much less pleasant than Egypt. They did not like foreign clothes or habits either and thought them to be unclean.

## Signs & Names

TO LEARN the language of ancient Egypt you must wait till you arrive. It was written in picture-signs; some showing the meanings of words, but others would also stand for sounds, as letters do. You will need a name. Here are some for girls: Meryt-Re, Iti, Nefertari and Nephret. 'Nefer' means lovely or excellent. It is found in boys' names too: Neferhotep, Hemon, Paneb and Kenna. Choose one, and begin your journey.

# YOUR MAP OF THE
## ANCIENT EGYPTIAN WORLD

THE PICTURE MAP opposite will help you to find the places which are mentioned in this book. You will see that all the towns lie close to a huge river, the Nile. Before it reaches the coast it splits into several branches which pour into the Mediterranean sea.

This great river was the source of ancient Egypt's prosperity. Every year, it over-flowed its banks and flooded a strip of land a few kilometres wide. You can see this area coloured green on the map. This was not a disaster, as you might think, but a great blessing to the Egyptians. Their land was a desert, with hardly any rain. The flood watered their soil (all at one go, but you will see that they skilfully made the flood water last all year) and when, after a few weeks, the river shrank again, it left behind a layer of dark mud which was extremely fertile.

If you are an experienced time-traveller you will know how different the world seems to people who have not been taught that there is a scientific reason for most things. We know today that a river floods because melting snow and heavy rain pour into it from very high mountains near its source. (The flood is now controlled by a modern dam.) The ancient Egyptians, however, would have laughed at such an explanation. They had not found the end of the river (it is over 4800 kms away) but they knew that the land south of their border was a scorching desert. It was obvious to them that the extraordinary behaviour of the river was caused by the gods. The gods sent this blessing because they were pleased with Egypt and its people. It was equally obvious to them that if the gods grew displeased they would no longer send the flood.

THE WORLD map (above) shows ancient Egypt's position in the African Continent. It was linked to its eastern neighbours by a short frontier which was easily defended. Attack was most likely from that direction. The people of the western desert were seldom a threat.

THE MEDITERRANEAN to the north was a helpful route for foreign imports. Sometimes it helped foreign invaders too. The southern boundary moved gradually further south as Egypt took control of the hot desert lands of Nubia and Kush (Sudan).

THE ANCIENT Egyptians thought that the entire sky was formed out of the body of the sky goddess, Nut, and that her father Shu, the air, parted her from her twin Geb, the earth, and lifted her up into place in the sky.

They believed that Egypt was the centre of the earth, the point where the world had come into being. A new pharaoh would have four birds released, to north, south, east and west, to tell the entire world a new reign had begun.

*Libyan trader*

*Hyena*

*Jackal*

*Gazelle*

DELTA

Border fort

Copper & lapis lazuli

Merchant

Bubastis

Giza

Heleopolis

Memphis

Stone

LOWER EGYPT

Bedouin tribes

Pharaoh out hunting

Tell el Amama

Copper & turquoise

THE NILE RIVER

WESTERN DESERT

Alabaster

EASTERN DESERT

Osiris

RED SEA

Abydos

Dendera    Karnak

Valley of the Kings

Thebes

Colossi

Gold quarrying

Nubians

Philae

NUBIA

Diorite quarrying

Crocodile

Abu Simbel

HERE AND ON the following page is a panorama of the world of ancient Egypt which awaits you. It is not meant to be a true-to-life picture, for you would not find all these things happening so close together. It is to act as your guide to this book. Start wherever you wish and follow the Q options.

A FEAST! What sort of foods did ancient Egyptians eat? How did they light the fire, and cook the food?
*Go to pages 18-19*

HOW DID the ancient Egyptians dress, and where did the cloth come from to make clothes?
*Go to pages 20-21*

HOW MANY rooms did an ancient Egyptian house have? Would there have been a garden?
*Go to pages 16-17*

WHAT SORT of life did Egyptian children lead? Will it matter if you are rich or poor, and how would you have been expected to behave?
*Go to pages 14-15*

WHAT IS THIS strange procession for and where is it going?
*Go to pages 40-41*

WHAT IS underneath this canopy? Is it a statue, is it a box – and just what is inside it?
*Go to pages 40-41*

WHAT SORT of life did priests have? Where did they fit into society?
*Go to pages 30-31*

# BEGIN YOUR NEW LIFE HERE

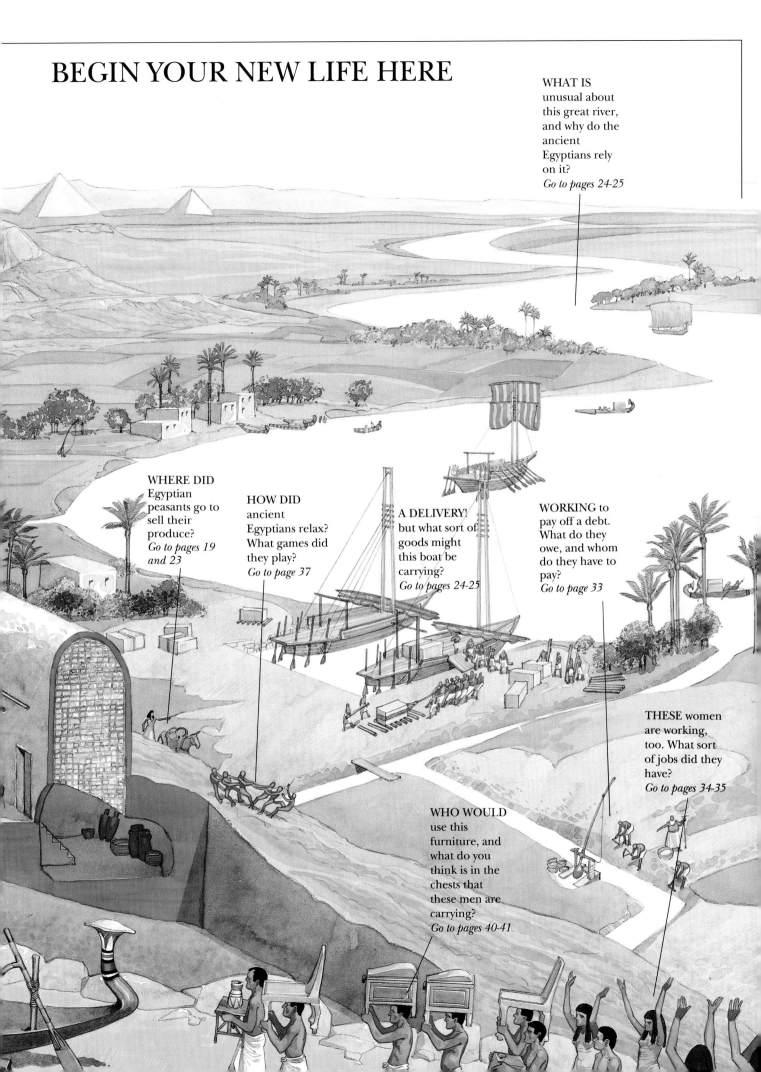

WHAT IS unusual about this great river, and why do the ancient Egyptians rely on it?
*Go to pages 24-25*

WHERE DID Egyptian peasants go to sell their produce?
*Go to pages 19 and 23*

HOW DID ancient Egyptians relax? What games did they play?
*Go to page 37*

A DELIVERY! but what sort of goods might this boat be carrying?
*Go to pages 24-25*

WORKING to pay off a debt. What do they owe, and whom do they have to pay?
*Go to page 33*

THESE women are working, too. What sort of jobs did they have?
*Go to pages 34-35*

WHO WOULD use this furniture, and what do you think is in the chests that these men are carrying?
*Go to pages 40-41*

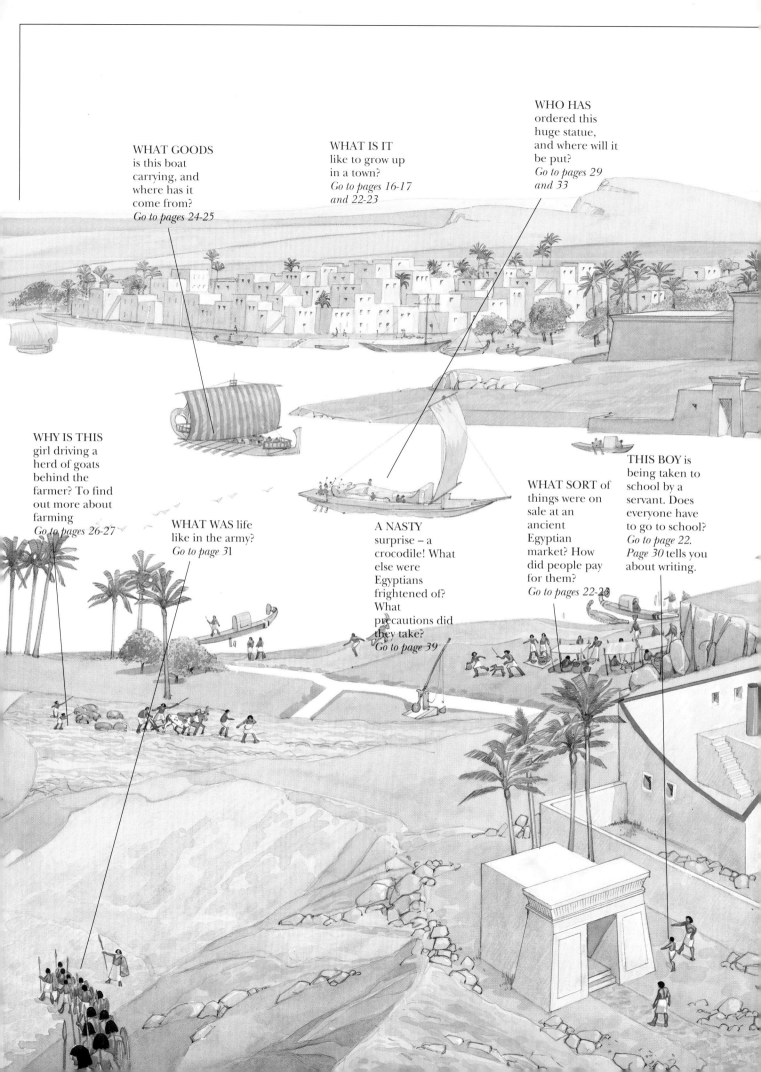

**WHAT GOODS** is this boat carrying, and where has it come from? *Go to pages 24-25*

**WHAT IS IT** like to grow up in a town? *Go to pages 16-17 and 22-23*

**WHO HAS** ordered this huge statue, and where will it be put? *Go to pages 29 and 33*

**WHY IS THIS** girl driving a herd of goats behind the farmer? To find out more about farming *Go to pages 26-27*

**WHAT WAS** life like in the army? *Go to page 31*

**A NASTY** surprise – a crocodile! What else were Egyptians frightened of? What precautions did they take? *Go to page 39*

**WHAT SORT** of things were on sale at an ancient Egyptian market? How did people pay for them? *Go to pages 22-23*

**THIS BOY** is being taken to school by a servant. Does everyone have to go to school? *Go to page 22. Page 30* tells you about writing.

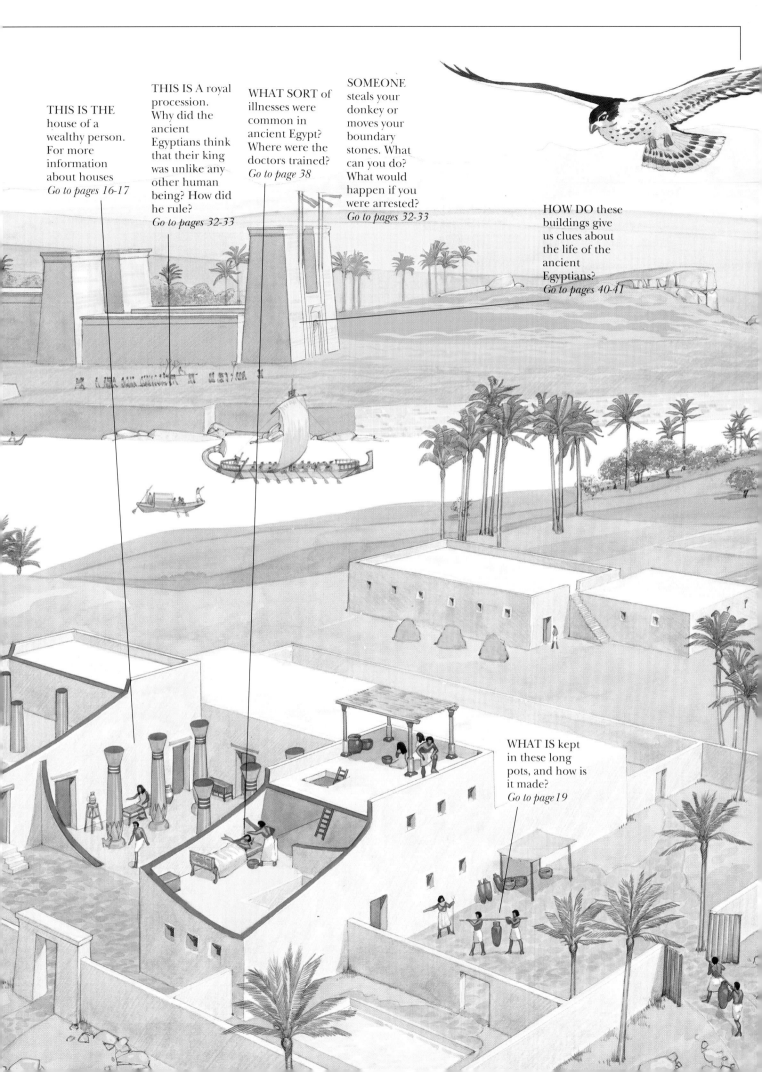

THIS IS THE house of a wealthy person. For more information about houses *Go to pages 16-17*

THIS IS A royal procession. Why did the ancient Egyptians think that their king was unlike any other human being? How did he rule? *Go to pages 32-33*

WHAT SORT of illnesses were common in ancient Egypt? Where were the doctors trained? *Go to page 38*

SOMEONE steals your donkey or moves your boundary stones. What can you do? What would happen if you were arrested? *Go to pages 32-33*

HOW DO these buildings give us clues about the life of the ancient Egyptians? *Go to pages 40-41*

WHAT IS kept in these long pots, and how is it made? *Go to page 19*

*You could decide whom you wished to marry, although elders would be expected to introduce suitable couples to each other.*

*After a wedding, husband and wife register the marriage contract made between them.*

*Presents that make up the bride's dowry (her possessions that she shares with her new husband) are carried from her father's house to her new home.*

*Bride and groom take offerings of food to the temple to ask the gods to bless their marriage.*

Q

*If you wanted to look your best, what could you use for make-up?*
*Go to page 35*

# YOUR FAMILY
## WHAT WOULD YOURS BE LIKE?

**W**HETHER YOUR PARENTS were rich or poor you probably had a loving happy childhood, with brothers and sisters. Ancient Egyptian families kept every baby that was born. Foreigners noticed this with surprise. In the ancient world, people living in lands where it was a struggle to survive often left babies to die because they could not afford to rear them. This was not necessary in Egypt, even for the poorest families. They did not need to buy clothes, for children ran about in the sun, and there would have been plenty of bread and fruit to eat. If you were really poor you could have lived on boiled papyrus roots for nothing.

*This fierce-looking creature is really a very kindly goddess. She is Tauert who protects pregnant women.*

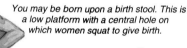

*Legend says that the creator god, Khnum, makes each person, together with his or her ka, upon his potter's wheel.*

*This symbol of two upraised arms represents the 'ka' spirit. Each person has a ka. It is part of you, born with you, and lives on after your death.*

*You may be born upon a birth stool. This is a low platform with a central hole on which women squat to give birth.*

*Reading the baby's stars. Let's hope you have been born on a lucky day!*

*While you are very young your mother will take you about in a pouch slung from her shoulders. She may breast-feed you until you are three.*

Your grandparents probably lived with you. In ancient Egypt old people were greatly respected. It was taken for granted that they were wiser than young people, for they had had much more time in which to learn. The Egyptians believed that if you could learn all the wisdom of the past you would then know all there was to know. They would not have understood the notion that by taking a fresh look at things people can make new discoveries about the world. Children were meant to do as they were told and were not encouraged to have ideas of their own.

*You leave babyhood behind and enter a new phase when you first wear clothes. Boys will put on a loin-cloth and belt, and girls will wear a dress.*

*Old people are well looked after. One pharaoh, hearing that a wise man was still fit at a 110, called him to be cared for at the palace.*

*You have an important duty to your parents. After their death you must take food to their tomb regularly so that their kas have nourishment.*

The Egyptians are very fond of children. People who have none are thought to be very unfortunate.

Your mother looked after you while you were too young to play with other children. Rich mothers had servants to mind their children. Working mothers carried their babies with them, to the fields, or the market, or wherever they had to go.

Wealthy families usually owned slaves. There were not many of these and they were mostly people captured in foreign wars. If your mother was a slave you might have been one as well, although you could have been made free-born. You could be beaten, or sold, but if you worked well, kind owners might reward you by giving you your freedom.

A childless man takes gifts to his relatives' tomb in the hope that they can persuade the gods to send a child.

The pharaoh and his queen often spend time with the royal children.

These are the queen's children. Like all boys of up to twelve years old, they have side-locks.

Couples wanting children might try the magic power of an amulet. This scarab-shaped one has the sun's life-giving power.

THIS FATHER (left) is a head craftsman who employs many workers. Though he must work hard his family live quite comfortably.

(ABOVE) the rich family of a high official. They have many servants, a big town house and country estates.

THE PEASANT FAMILY on the right live in a tiny house. They have a few animals and grow food on a small patch of land. They do not own the house or land. The village belongs to a rich land owner. The family pay rent in the form of hard work in the owner's fields.

If none of these methods produces results, a couple can adopt a child by coming to an agreement with its parents.

### DIVORCE

If a wife is ill-treated by her husband she can ask her relatives to assist her by appealing to a judge for help.

A judge can tell a husband to improve his behaviour. One man was told he'd receive a hundred lashes if he continued his cruelty.

Divorce is quite simple. The couple make a declaration before witnesses. Both may then remarry. The wife usually has the children.

Q

You are planning a feast! How could you make beer and wine for your guests?
*Go to pages 18-19*

# YOUR HOUSE
## WHAT SORT OF HOUSE WOULD YOU LIVE IN?

Bricks are made from a mixture of mud and chopped straw. They are shaped in moulds and baked hard in the sun.

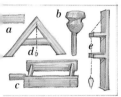

Some tools: **a.** set-square; **b.** mallet; **c.** brick-mould; **d.** plumb-line for checking horizontal surfaces and **e.** another for vertical.

All houses, even the pharaoh's dazzling palace, are made of mud. Only temples and tombs are built of stone.

Strong beams often have to be imported, as palm trunks are too flexible. Egypt is short of good timber.

### Q
When would you first wear clothes?
Go to page 14

**T**HIS IS THE KIND of house you might have lived in if your parents were working people, not rich but not poor either. It was joined to other houses on either side, and similar houses lined both sides of the street. Some town houses were two or three storeys high. In poor parts these would often have been crammed with several families. There was a shortage of land for town houses, for nobody wanted to live in the desert and the fertile land near the river was needed to grow food.

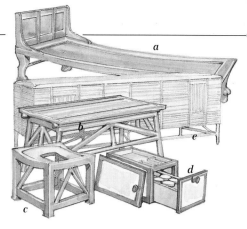

Furniture: **a.** a bed with a foot-board **b.** a side table; **c.** a lavatory seat to be placed over a pot; **d.** a toilet box with compartments for cosmetic jars and a mirror; **e.** a sideboard.

Windows are square holes in the walls. Some have brickwork grills to soften the sun's glare.

*Vent for light and air*

*Niches for sacred images*

HOUSES MAY soon need repair, especially if flood water reaches the foundations. Some are built on raised platforms to prevent this. Rats are a nuisance, too. They gnaw holes in the walls.

ROOF timbers are covered with thatch or matting and topped with a thick layer of mud plaster.

**THE VIEW FROM A SMALLER HOUSE**

Windows are small and high, to keep out dust, heat and glare. If you peer out of the window in your house what are you likely to see outside?

If your house is near the town centre there will be lots going on. Traders put up stalls all along the road, leaving little room for the traffic.

Sounds of bargaining and a rich medley of smells rise up to you. Porters deliver wine, women bring water from the well, officials push through the crowd.

The houses might have seemed bare to us, with just a few stools and some small tables on which dishes and drinking vessels could be placed for meals. There were no cupboards. Possessions were kept in wooden chests, baskets and jars. An ordinary family might have only one bed, or none. People would sleep on the floor or the roof, on mats, although the danger from scorpions made them raise their heads on a headrest.

The rooms were whitewashed or painted, often with blue or yellow walls. The floors were of beaten earth. One room would be fitted with an altar in a shrine-like enclosure, for family worship of a friendly household god, such as Bes or Tauert. Grander houses had more rooms, with tiled floors, coloured ceilings, and walls with gaily painted borders of ducks and lotus petals.

IF YOUR HOUSE is in the country you are likely to be either very rich or very poor. Often peasant homes have only one room which all the family must share.

*Cities have many avenues of fine buildings, but working people are crammed into packed, unplanned streets.*

*Where do you go if you want space for a game? City children use the roof-tops and run from one to another.*

*Wall of the village*

*Light roofing of branches and straw*

*Storage jars*

*Cellar*

*Oven*

*Mortar, for pounding grain, set into the floor*

*Kitchen*

*Bedroom and storeroom*

*A wealthy house has guest rooms, a set of private rooms for the owner and another for the women of the house.*

**A VIEW FROM THE GARDEN WINDOW OF A LARGE HOUSE**

*If your parents are members of the pharaoh's court, your town house would have many cool colonnaded rooms and a large garden.*

*Your window will look out over neat paths, rectangular pools and small garden pavilions. Many gardeners are needed to train the plants and keep them watered.*

*The garden is very peaceful. A high wall keeps out noise and intruders. A gatekeeper guards the entrance and only lets in friends and official visitors.*

*It will have a garden with a pool to swim in. When the family go to their country house, the children have even more space to enjoy.*

Q

The festival of the local god is coming up. What will it be like?
*Go to page 37*

# FOOD & DRINK
## WHAT WOULD YOU EAT AND DRINK?

First make some flour by grinding grain to a powder by pushing it back and forth between two stones.

The grinding is easier if you add a little grit to the grain. Then mix the flour with water to form a dough.

Add some honey to the mixture if you want to make sweet bread. Shape the dough into loaves.

Bake the loaves in an oven if you have one. If not you can cook the dough in pots stacked over a fire.

Q

Your neighbour's wife is a gleaner. What does this mean?
*Go to page 34*

THE ANCIENT EGYPTIANS had the good luck to live in a sunny land where the soil was just right for growing crops. If your family was very poor your diet of bread, beans, onions and green vegetables might have become boring, but at least you would not have been hungry. When the grain harvest was good, government officials stored wheat and barley in granaries belonging to the pharaoh, so that it could be shared out with everybody in years when the crop was poor. Beef was the meat that the Egyptians enjoyed most, if they could afford it. It was expensive because cattle needed fields of grass to eat and that took up precious land. People thought that mutton and goat were not so good, and pork and fish were considered unclean. However, most people ate a lot of fish and poultry because they were the cheapest meats to buy. If you caught a lot of fish or wild birds you gutted them and hung them to dry in the sun. Then they would keep for a long time.

Grilling a goose over a brazier of burning charcoal, which has to be fanned to give a good heat. Meat is also spit-roasted, or stewed in pots. Cooking is often done out-of-doors. There is not much chance of rain.

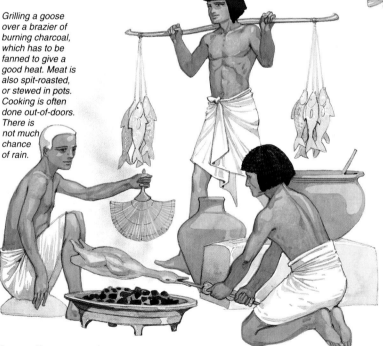

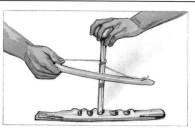

FIRE-MAKING, using a bow drill, a piece of wood with a row of holes, and a hard stick that just fits them. Press the stick into a hole and rotate it fast with the drill. The woods rubbing together produce a spark.

IN THE COUNTRY you have to know how to slaughter an animal if you want meat. In the towns there are butchers to do this for you. The animal's legs are roped together and it is pulled onto its side to be killed.

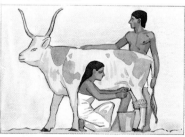

Only wealthy landowners can afford to keep large herds of cattle and kill them for eating.

Cattle are mainly used for ploughing and giving milk. Milk goes sour in the heat so most is made into curd cheese.

**MAKING BEER**

How to make beer. Crumble half-cooked barley bread into a vat.

Add water that has been sweetened with dates. This will soon ferment.

Expect the liquid to be very lumpy. You will need to strain it into jars.

Seal the tops of the jars firmly with clay and store them in a cool place.

The beer will still be rather thick and you may need to strain it again.

Some people drink it straight from the jar through a drinking tube.

(Left) some kitchen equipment: **a.** a storage bowl, **b.** a fruit basket **c.** two drinking cups and **d.** a wine jar. The jar's pointed base will need to be put in a stand.

Cooking was usually done at the back of the house, to keep smoke and smells out. Poor people who had just one room cooked over a fire made in a hole in the floor.

Wealthy Egyptians had servants to cook and serve meals. At large meals the hosts and important guests sat on low chairs. Children and other people used cushions or mats. Servants brought in the courses one by one and put them on small tables beside the diners – dishes of roast meat seasoned with garlic, salads, cucumber, leeks, lots of bread and sticky cakes, and plates of delicious melons and figs. People ate with their fingers, and rinsed them in water between courses. You might have missed being able to eat oranges and bananas while in ancient Egypt. Like lemons, pears, peaches and cherries, these fruits were unknown.

## WHAT CAN YOU EAT?

A wide variety of vegetables is grown. Prosperous peasants have their own vegetable patches.

Pigeons, crane, teal, geese and ducks are reared for eating. Food is forced into some birds to fatten them.

You can buy food at the local market where country people sell what they do not need for themselves.

As well as growing or buying food, you can hunt and fish for it. This is the way poor people get some delicacies.

Bee-keepers taking honeycombs from round pottery beehives. The one on the left is puffing smoke at the bees to calm them (this is still done today!). Honey is also collected from wild bees in the desert.

Musicians entertain a wealthy couple and their guests while they eat. The meal is nearly over, for servants have placed fruit beside each diner. The women wear cones of refreshing scented wax upon their heads.

### MAKING WINE

Though beer is the most popular drink, wine is made too. There are vineyards in the Delta, which is at the mouth of the Nile River, and grape vines are often grown on trellises in large gardens.

The ripe grapes are put in a big trough. Treaders, clinging to ropes to keep their balance, press out the juice with their bare feet.

The juice is poured into jars to ferment. When fermentation stops the jars are sealed and dated, and the wine is left to mature.

Q

You have become an official mourner. What will you have to do?
*Go to page 35*

# YOUR CLOTHES
## W H A T   W O U L D   Y O U   W E A R ?

Flax is harvested by being pulled out of the ground, not cut. This back-breaking work is done mostly by men.

Flax harvest, from a wall-painting. Half-ripe stems make the best thread. If they are too ripe and soft they will only be fit for mats and rope.

*Spindle*

*Stripper*

The stems are soaked for several days to separate the fibres which are then beaten until they are soft.

**(Above)** a spindle, and a stripper for pulling off flax seeds. A man holds one down with his foot in the scene **(top right).**

The spinner fixes fibres to the spindle and twists them into a strong thread as she lets the spindle drop.

A
S AN ANCIENT Egyptian you would have taken a lot of care over your appearance. Fashion today, which consists of knowing what the latest trend is, and wearing it casually, is the exact opposite of the ancient Egyptian way of dressing. Egyptian clothes hardly altered over hundreds of years, so you could not make an impression by wearing a new style. Instead, people took pride in keeping themselves and their clothes spotlessly clean and neatly arranged at all times.

Men's loin-cloths. **(Above left)** a worker's simple version; **(centre)** a wrapped skirt; **(right)** an upper-class style, made of finely pleated linen tied in a large loop falling to the knee. **(Left)** a loin-cloth of gazelle skin. It is covered all over in tiny slits, apart from on the border and centre panel, in order to make the leather supple and cool to wear.

If you do no heavy work you can stay cool and fresh in a robe of thinnest linen **(left)**, sashed with a huge pleated belt.

Clothes were almost always made of linen, which is woven from fibres of the flax plant. The ancient Egyptians were famous for their weaving. Workers wore practical loin-cloths or simple tunic dresses. People often worked naked; servant girls sometimes wore just a belt. Better off people wore wide garments of transparent white cloth, which was pleated, draped and tied. Both men and women made up their eyes and lips and wore black wigs of wool or hair.

Weaving is done on a loom which is a frame made of two beams and held by four pegs driven into the ground.

**GETTING DRESSED**

Q

You have heard people saying that the flood is coming. What will happen?
*Go to page 24*

What's it like to live on the river?
*Go to page 25*

You do not dress without washing first. Wealthy homes have a tiled wash area where water is poured over you.

This woman lives in comfort. When her maid has bathed her she rubs herself all over with scented oil.

Over a narrow shift she places a large rectangle of transparent linen with a central hole for her head.

She drapes the cloth carefully, draws its fulness together below her chest and fastens it in a knot.

She takes powdered mineral colours from little jars and mixes them with oils, to make up her face.

Her maid produces today's wig, made of human hair. Elaborately curled wigs are worn on special occasions.

Whether you are rich or poor you will wear rings, necklaces and ear-studs. They may be of gold, or just beads.

(BELOW) essential toilet articles; **a.** tweezers for plucking out unwanted hair, **b.** a razor and **c.** a comb.

*a*

*b*

*c*

Priests follow strict rules of cleanliness. Each must wash several times a day, and shave his head.

He must remove all body hair in order to be pure enough to approach the god. He plucks it out with tweezers or shaves.

He puts on freshly washed linen. He may not wear wool or sandals of leather. These are considered unclean.

His leopard-skin robe shows that he serves the great god Amun. In many cults the priests wear no wig.

*a*

*c*

*b*

**(Above) a.** a mirror of burnished copper, **b.** a double cosmetic holder and **c.** another in the form of a girl with a duck.

**(Left)** a high official and his wife. Rich people do not show their wealth by wearing gorgeously patterned clothes or exaggerated styles. They wear the finest transparent white linen gauze, which is very expensive as everyone knows, and they hang fortunes around their necks in the form of gold necklaces set with turquoise and lapis lazuli stones.

**WASHING LINEN**

White linen clothes need constant laundering. If you wash your own you will find it easiest to do this by the river or canal. You rinse them, pound them on a stone and bleach them in the sun.

Putting back the pleats. Very thin linen garments are often finely pleated. They have to be re-pleated every time they are washed. The damp cloth is pressed into grooves in a wooden board and left to dry.

Sandals – sole, upper and side views. The sandals on the left are ones made of plaited papyrus, and right, of palm fibre. It is usual to walk barefoot, and carry your sandals, wearing them only when necessary.

Q You have just built a new house. What sort of roof should you put on it?
*Go to page 16*

# LIVING IN A TOWN
## WHAT WOULD YOUR LIFE BE LIKE?

*If your parents want
you to have a
career they will
certainly send you
to school. Your
mother gives you
your lunch.*

*Some schools are
run by priests. Both
boys and girls start
going when they are
quite young, but
girls will stay at
home when they
turn 12 years old.*

*Plastered boards or
flakes of stone are
used to write on.
You have to do a
lot of copying out
and dictation.*

*Lessons are based
on learning the
wise teachings of
past writers. If you
do not listen you will
be beaten.*

Q

If you wanted to
cook a goose,
why would a
bow-drill come
in handy?
*Go to page 18*

How did the
world begin?
*Go to page 36*

PERHAPS YOU MIGHT have grown up in one
of the big cities on the Nile. Egypt was divided
into regions, called nomes, each having a
local capital. Over the centuries the pharaohs
moved their capital city from one place to another. In
the period described in this book, the capital was the
splendid city of Thebes.

In the cities, some people lived in poverty and
others in amazing luxury. Many buildings were huge
and splendidly decorated. There were temples with
painted walls and enormous gates flanked by gold-
tipped obelisks which flashed in the sunlight. All the
temples and the great palace of the pharaoh were
ringed by high walls, above which one saw the tops of
palm trees which shaded vast gardens.

(BELOW) THE CITY comes to the
edge of the water. The river-side
road leads through the port area,
where boats are unloaded, past
temples (you can see a temple
gateway), workshops and houses.
Many markets, large and small, line
the waterfront.

**LEARNING AT
HOME**

*If your parents are poor they may send you to
school for a few years, but they will not be
able to afford to keep you there for long. You
will have to earn a living as soon as possible.
This boy is going to be a sandal-maker like,
his father.*

*He has had to leave school to start working
for his father who will teach him all the skills
of his trade. He learns to cut and sew leather,
to weave soles of papyrus or palm fibre and
to pull the toe-thongs through.*

*The finished sandals are sold from a stall
which the family sets up in the street outside
the house. Getting good value for your work
can be tricky. This trainee is learning the art
of bartering.*

You might have lived in a narrow, crooked, stinking alley, but you could have walked along highways which were lined with sphinxes, and avenues of imposing government buildings, vast granaries and storehouses. The streets were packed with people scurrying on urgent business – merchants arriving from the port, temple messengers, craftsmen delivering goods – soldiers marching, and great lords carried by on litters covered in gold. People who had the time gossiped, joked and stared.

## IN THE MARKET

*A cloth merchant shows the quality of his goods. No one makes finer linen than the Egyptians.*

*Slaves, usually prisoners-of-war, are expensive to buy. The price is agreed in writing, to avoid arguments.*

*The sun is scorching hot, the shade is hot and dusty. You need to stop at a drink stall before you face the walk home.*

*Lots of men are shopping for food. They are probably kitchen staff from rich houses, who are buying supplies.*

## GOING SHOPPING

*Your mother wants to buy some fish. She cannot pay for it with coins, for Egyptians do not use money. She has to give the fishmonger something in exchange for his fish, so she makes some fig cakes.*

*She sets off for market carrying a big basket of cakes. She has made enough to buy some vegetables as well. Traders will accept the cakes if they need them or if they think they can use them to buy something else.*

*How many cakes is a fish worth? That is when the bargaining begins! Shopping can take a lot of time. To buy something costly, like an ox, you must have lots to offer – linen, necklaces and bags of grain, perhaps.*

**Q**

Everybody is talking about the man who died abroad. Why is this so terrible?
*Go to page 39*

# ON THE RIVER
## WHAT SORT OF SIGHTS WOULD YOU SEE?

*Each year's high water is marked on a gauge. Anxious officials watch it to judge how high the flood will be this time.*

*Officials tell the Head of Irrigation how far the water has risen each day and he reports this daily to the pharaoh.*

*Soon water covers a strip about five kilometres wide on each bank. The villages are built on higher ground but some become islands.*

*A criss-cross of canals has been prepared. These fill with water which cannot drain away when the flood sinks.*

Q

You have to write a very important letter. What could you use to do this?
*Go to page 30*

THE NILE WAS ancient Egypt's great highway. People sometimes needed to make lengthy journeys up and down the long narrow land. The pharaoh's messengers, for instance, speeding with instructions to the rulers of the nomes, or pilgrims making their way to the city of Abydos where the body of the much loved god Osiris was believed to be buried (a journey everyone hoped to make at least once in their life). Roads could not be built on flooded land, or in the sandy desert. Travellers and goods of every kind travelled by river.

The journey was a pleasant one. The wind, coming from the north, helped boats to make the upstream journey. Downstream they were carried by the current. It was agreeable to watch the villages and temples slip past. Sometimes you passed enormous seated statues which gazed across the river into the desert.

THIS IS HOW the Egyptians imagine that Hapi, the Nile god, looks. He is holding a dish loaded with fruit and ducks which are an offering. Lotus flowers hang from his arm and he grasps tall papyrus stems.

### A DAY IN THE LIFE OF THE RIVER

*DAYBREAK. People are only just beginning to wake up and stir. At this early hour the river is quiet and belongs to the wild creatures. If you look closely you can see a log floating by, or could it be a hungry crocodile?*

*EARLY MORNING. Customs officials arrive at the quayside punctually, before the first boat is unloaded. They make a note of each item of cargo as it is carried ashore. The shippers must pay tax on the goods.*

*NOON. Traders have set out stalls on the crowded quay. It is a good place to do business. Sailors come ashore with sacks of grain, which are their wages. They want to spend part of it on goods from the food stalls.*

On your journey you passed the boats of humble local traders, with mat-covered cabins and patched brown sails. Or brightly painted slender pleasure boats, with dainty pavilions to sit in. Or private yachts, with twelve oarsmen on each side, and pillared cabins with luggage stowed on the roof. Long distance vessels would pass on their way to the Delta, with gold from the eastern desert, and ivory and gemstones from Nubia. Foreign ships brought in timber from Lebanon and ingots of Syrian bronze.

*(Below) an Egyptian cargo boat, with a stern shaped like a lotus flower, has lowered sail, ready to unload. Because of its size its hull needs to be braced by a long rope. All sorts of produce travels by river; corn and cattle, fruit, vegetables, sacks of lentils and casks of dried fish, animal skins, papyrus and bales of linen.*

*The stems of the papyrus plant are harvested in the marshy Delta, where it grows along the river's edge.*

*You can make a good cheap boat from papyrus. Lash the stems tightly to make them watertight.*

*There is good hunting in the marshes, but it could be a dangerous sport.*

*Herdsmen have to take extra care of their cattle in the wet season and guide them over flooded ground.*

*AFTERNOON. A rich official is setting off to spend some days at his country estate. His private boat, with an elegant awning and cushions, is waiting for him. The horses for his hunting chariot are being led on board.*

*EARLY EVENING. Fishermen are bringing in their catch. They stretch huge weighted nets out into the river and drive the fish towards them. Several men are needed to scoop up each net as they are heavy with fish.*

*DUSK. Music and laughter float over the water as a boat draws to shore. Perhaps its cheerful passengers have been holding a river party, or perhaps they are pilgrims pausing for the night on their way to Abydos.*

**Q**

If you were blind what could you do for a living?
*Go to page 38*

Why did people live in fear of locusts!?
*Go to page 39*

*If you are a busy
official you will only
have time to visit
your country estate
for short spells now
and then.*

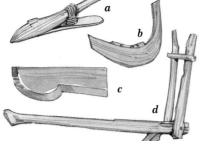

YOU MUST MAKE your own farm
tools out of wood. **(Above) a.** a
mattock; **b.** a flint-bladed sickle;
**c.** a winnowing scoop; **d.** a plough.

# LIVING AS A FARMER
## WHAT USE COULD YOU MAKE OF THE LAND?

THE ANCIENT EGYPTIANS divided the year into
three seasons of four months each. The first,
beginning in June, was the flood season. The
start of this season was an anxious time for
everyone. Until they saw the level of the water rising up
the river bank they could not be certain that Hapi, the
river god, would still take care of Egypt. When the flood
was at its height there were thanksgiving ceremonies.

The next season was the growing season. The main
crops were wheat and barley. Ploughing was simple,
since the new layer of mud had no stones or weeds in it.
By the time the crops began to sprout, the mud was dry
and needed water. Every field had a ditch linked to a
canal. The mouth of the ditch was opened and water
ran in.

The last season was harvest time. This was also the
season for repairing the canals, which were dry by then,
ready for the next flood.

*On arrival you
check that your
overseer has been
running the farm
workshops well
and making a profit
for you.*

YOUR CATTLE COULD be stolen
if they are not marked. **(Above)**
branding a cow. **(Below)** digging
fields by hand, an old method still
used by peasants too poor to own
an ox, or by owners rich enough to
have many labourers.

*You drive out to the
harvest field to see
that the reapers
work well and do
not leave a lot for
the gleaners.*

*To make the most
of your visit you
could go hunting for
antelope in the
desert beyond
the hills.*

**THE FARMING YEAR**

Q

You've had to
leave school to
work with your
father. What
sort of things
will you learn?
*Go to page 22*

*Plough the soft mud
as soon as the
floods go down,
before the sun has
time to bake the
earth.*

*With a helper
behind you to
scatter the seed,
and your goats to
trample it in, the job
is soon done.*

*Tending the crops
needs more care.
There is no rain so
they must be
watered. Watch out
for greedy birds!*

*Let's hope you can
afford to keep a few
animals – some
goats, a pig and
some ducks and
geese, perhaps.*

*You may not be
able to harvest your
corn when you like.
If you have a land-
lord he may make
you cut his first.*

*The corn is cut just
below the ear. The
sheaves are then
bound together and
carried home in a
net basket.*

If your only cow is sick, or you have to sell her, you will have to pull the plough yourself.

In theory all the land in Egypt belonged to the pharaoh. In practice all pharaohs in the past had rewarded their high officials by letting them have land. The land originally went with the job, but jobs tended to be handed down in families and in this way some people came to have large estates and to control all the peasants who farmed on that land. A lot of the land belonged to temples, given to them by past pharaohs in honour of the gods.

**(Above)** counting cattle. Herdsmen drive them past the overseer. As he counts them his scribes write down the size of each herd and the number of new calves born. Only rich owners can afford to keep such big beef herds.

Peasant farmers breed birds for eggs and meat, and to take to market to sell.

Each year poor people must do forced labour for the pharaoh. You have to repair the canals, before the flood.

Life is full of misfortunes. Your donkey nibbles someone's crop and he threatens to take you to court.

**(Below)** a shaduf – which is a pole with a bucket and counterweight – will help you swing water from the canal into your field.

A granary. The grain is tipped into the granary at the top and taken out through push-up doors at the bottom.

Tax officials come to take the grain they say you owe. Your crop has failed and you cannot pay, so they beat you.

The grain has to be dislodged from the ears of corn. The simplest way is to get farm animals to trample it out.

Winnowing. The grain is still mixed with bits of husk and straw. Toss it in the air and the breeze will blow the bits away.

Fig trees and vines give you fruit. You could try newer crops from abroad, such as pomegranates.

At the height of summer the land is shrivelled and the canals are dry. Then once again the flood returns.

Soon your fields are under water. You go fishing to get extra food, and also to have something to sell.

While the flood halts work you should be mending tools and making new ones, ready for the new season.

## Q

How could you prove that an official document was authentic?
*Go to page 32*

How important was the pharaoh?
*Go to page 32*

# IN THE WORKSHOPS
### W H A T   C O U L D   Y O U   M A K E ?

Workers delivering bronze ingots. Bronze, a mixture of copper and tin, is found in parts of Asia, or it can be made.

The metal is melted over charcoal-burning furnaces. Bellows, worked by foot, intensify the heat.

The bellows have long reed nozzles which soon get scorched. These men are bringing replacements.

Metal needing to be melted is held over the fire in a pottery crucible, by means of flexible rods.

Casting a large object. Molten metal is poured into a pottery mould through a row of funnels. This must be done fast to get an even result. When the metal is cold the mould will be taken apart. This mould is for a bronze door.

Molten glass is blown, or cast in moulds. Glass beads, and jewellery inlaid with glass are popular. Craftsmen are also skilled in making faience - a glass-like substance formed by firing finely-powdered quartz.

Craftsmen in a temple workshop are putting the finishing touches to a shrine. It has been ornamented with painted carvings and gold leaf. A shrine is the house of a god, so only the best is good enough.

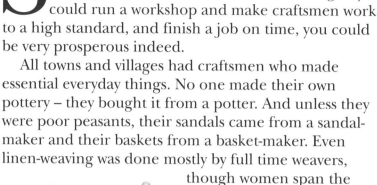

S KILLED CRAFTSMEN WERE always in demand in ancient Egypt. If you were good at using your hands you were sure of a reasonable living. If you could run a workshop and make craftsmen work to a high standard, and finish a job on time, you could be very prosperous indeed.

All towns and villages had craftsmen who made essential everyday things. No one made their own pottery – they bought it from a potter. And unless they were poor peasants, their sandals came from a sandal-maker and their baskets from a basket-maker. Even linen-weaving was done mostly by full time weavers, though women span the thread at home. These were humble crafts compared with the work done for the pharaoh and the priests. Jewellers, bronze-casters, stone masons, goldsmiths, sculptors and painters worked constantly on the pharaoh's palaces and tomb, and in the temple workshops.

Shaping and decorating vessels of beaten metal. The worker in the foreground is making a bowl from a sheet of metal by hammering it into shape over an anvil. His companion is making an inscription onto a vase by a method called chasing.

You go to a potter for storage jars, cooking pots, and serving vessels of all kinds. The potter has to keep the wheel spinning with his left hand while he shapes the clay with his right.

Fibre brush     Tool basket

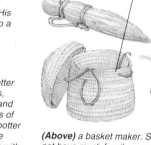

(Above) a basket maker. Since homes do not have much furniture you will find basketwork containers the answer to storage problems. They can be made from rushes, papyrus or date-palm fibres.

Q
You have seen a market official walking around with a baboon. Is this his pet?
Go to page 33

**CARPENTRY**

Large pieces of timber are split with an axe into roughly the size needed.

Sawing planks. The wood is held firm by tying it to a post. Pull the saw to cut. Don't push it like a modern one.

Wood is smoothed with an adze. Its bronze blade is tied on. (You will have to manage without a plane.)

Checking the work. This man has been smoothing a plank. Now he uses a straight-edge to check his accuracy.

Using a light saw. Brace the wood against your foot, and push on the top end, as you pull on the saw.

Mortises are cut with a bronze chisel. Bronze is not very hard, so you will have to re-sharpen frequently.

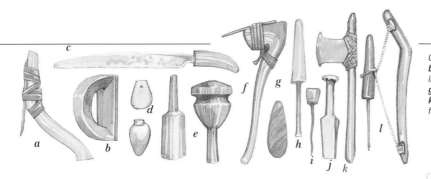

## GOLDSMITHING

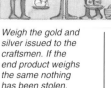

Weigh the gold and silver issued to the craftsmen. If the end product weighs the same nothing has been stolen.

These workers made magnificent coloured and gilded statues, gold vessels, wall paintings, and exquisite furniture in precious woods. There was always work to do, for each pharaoh ordered new temples to be built, or enlarged existing ones, with bigger courtyards, loftier pillars, and yet more splendid furnishings. Huge riverboats left the quarries, loaded with building stone and gigantic statues for these projects. All this was done for the glory of the gods and of the pharaoh who was himself a god.

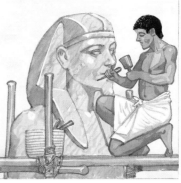

A skilled mason finishes a statue. To avoid shifting unnecessarily large blocks of stone, huge statues are often roughly cut to shape at the quarry. Details are chiselled later. **(Below)**, a caricature of a workmate.

Beating gold. Put a cushion beneath the work to give a soft support. For gilding, the gold must be beaten leaf-thin.

Joining a vessel made in two pieces is a tricky job. Use a metal that melts easily to join them together.

A chariot maker's workshop. The body of the chariot is made of wicker. You are not likely to own a chariot unless you are very wealthy. They are quite a new luxury for the ancient Egyptians. Not so long ago they had no horses to pull them. Horses and chariots were brought to Egypt by Asian invaders in about 1600 BC.

Asians ride horses, but the ancient Egyptians have not taken up that idea.

Make sure that you support large vessels carefully while you give them their final polish.

### FURNITURE MAKING

Ornamenting a shrine with cut-out amulets. They are roughed out with an adze and finished with a chisel.

Keep a pot of glue heated, ready for sticking on veneers of decorative wood, or for attaching gold leaf to a carefully smoothed surface.

Fine objects for rich clients are often gilded. You can make the gold glitter by rubbing it with a smooth stone.

For a good finish the wood has to be rubbed and polished. This worker is smoothing down a column.

This man is using a bow-drill to make holes through which rushes will be threaded, and woven into a seat.

Bed-frame making. The mattress goes over a strong mesh of interwoven ropes. These men are drilling the holes for the ropes.

Q

Last night you dreamed that you had the face of a leopard. What does this mean?
*Go to page 39*

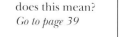

For important writing, paper is used. It is made from papyrus reed. Tall young stems, freshly cut, are needed.

The rind is peeled from the stems. The soft pith inside is cut into strips which are laid side by side.

More pith is laid at right angles and pounded with a mallet. It dries as a tough sheet. These sheets are joined into rolls.

If you cannot write you can dictate a letter to the local letter writer. He is a very lowly scribe.

HIEROGLYPHS of the type used for inscriptions. For everyday work people use a more joined-up version which is quicker to write. You sit cross-legged (below) to write with the papyrus on your lap, unrolling what you need.

**(Below) a.** a pot for grinding pigment and **b.** a brush holder.

*a*

*b*

**(Right)** the hieroglyph for 'writing', formed of a brush, pigment bag and palette.

**(Right)** a temple, cut away to show its interior. Each town has a temple dedicated to an important local god. It is the centre of a large estate, with farms and workshops to provide everything that the priests and the god need. You probably know the surroundings of your local temple quite well, but unless you are a priest or priestess you cannot enter the temple itself.

# C A R E E R S
## WHAT OPTIONS WOULD BE OPEN TO YOU?

O FFICIALS KEPT WRITTEN records, so in all careers you started as a scribe (a professional writer). Then, if you knew the right people you could become a priest or army officer.

Your employer wouldn't necessarily be pleased if you said that you had a good idea. That was not expected of you. A clever scribe made it seem that his master had thought of it. His master might mention it to the pharaoh, but always as if the pharaoh had had the idea. The pharaoh got the credit, and the scribe might get a reward.

Priests offering incense to the statue of a god. If you become a very high ranking priest you may do this.

It is a very sacred duty. You will be acting as the pharaoh's deputy, for in theory only he can serve the gods.

*Side chambers*

*Pillared inner courtyard*

*Sanctuary containing shrine*

**GETTING AHEAD**

Q

What would you see if you looked out of your window in a town house?

*Go to page 16*

Perhaps, through the influence of a family friend, you become a scribe in the law courts. You work hard and are so respectful to your masters that you rise to being Superintendent of Documents of the supreme court.

Perhaps you are very good at organising things. You could start work as scribe to the Commander of the Army and eventually become his chief advisor. He praises you to the pharaoh who makes you the Governor of a province.

If you are a very ambitious person, you could always make yourself so useful to the pharaoh and impress him so much that he would decide to make you his vizier, or Chief Minister. It is not very likely, but it is not impossible!

(Left) the pharaoh in his battle chariot. Chariots need a crew of two – one to drive and one to fight. (Right) the battle standards of various regiments.

You might find yourself in the army unwillingly. Scribes are sent to the villages to conscript men.

The temples employed many people. They needed priests to serve the gods, and officials to run the farms and workshops of the temple estates. The army was also an excellent career if you could afford a horse and chariot, for officers bought their own. Life as an ordinary soldier was hard, though it gave a reasonable living. The pharaohs of the New Kingdom were more warlike than those of the past and kept a permanent army.

(RIGHT) AN INFANTRYMAN.
Below are some weapons: **a.** and **b.** swords; **c.** lancehead; **d.** dagger; **e.** club with hand guard; **f.** battle-axe; **g.** club with projecting blade.

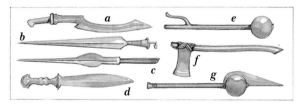

Like all Egyptian organisations the army needs lots of scribes. Every fact is noted. The best way to find out the number of enemy dead is to cut off the right hands and count them.

A slinger. His catapult can hurl a stone many metres. Slingers are useful attackers in siege warfare.

You may do lots of heavy work, like hauling building material for the huge temples which the pharaohs order.

Archer and spear-man. A big wooden shield protects your body, and perhaps a leather tunic reinforced with metal.

Weapons are issued at the start of a campaign, in a ceremony before the pharaoh. You file up to receive yours.

After the opening chariot charge the infantry attack, first with spears and then by hand-to-hand combat with daggers.

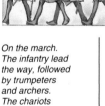

On the march. The infantry lead the way, followed by trumpeters and archers. The chariots follow behind.

**WARFARE**

The pharaoh is leading his army on campaign. He has decided to camp for the night. The soldiers swiftly make an enclosure with their shields. They then unload supplies and put up tents – a very large one for the pharaoh.

A siege. The enemy shoot arrows, and fling javelins and stones as you try to scale their fortress with ladders. You may well be killed, but the thought of the grain, wine and weapons you can seize if you win spurs you on.

Officers who serve the pharaoh long and bravely are rewarded with gold, land and high positions. You might be honoured like this Chief Standard Bearer. At an official ceremony he is being appointed Head of Police.

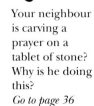

Q
Your neighbour is carving a prayer on a tablet of stone? Why is he doing this?
Go to page 36

*First the pharaoh offers worship to the gods. This is his duty. Egypt will not prosper if he fails to please them.*

*During the morning the pharaoh hears his vizier's daily report and decides on all important matters arising from it.*

*In the afternoon he inspects work on a huge new temple. Like past pharaohs, he is building one to gratify the gods.*

*The day may end with a feast for a foreign ambassador or perhaps the pharaoh can spend time with the queen.*

Q

You've taken a trip into town and seen lots of busy craftsmen. Do they make a good living?
*Go to pages 28-29*

# PHARAOHS AND LAWS
## HOW WOULD YOUR LIFE BE RULED?

*The pharaoh marks official documents with this royal seal to prove they come from him. It shows his name surrounded with sacred symbols.*

NO ONE WAS more important than the pharaoh. You were more anxious about his welfare and keener to obey him than any present day subject would be. The pharaoh was a god on earth. While he reigned he was Horus, the son of Re the sun god, in human form. When he died he was united with the sun god, and the next pharaoh became a new Horus. The pharaoh was all-powerful and all-knowing, and ruled everyone's fate. He ruled the government and law courts, was chief priest of the temples, headed the army and controlled trade, irrigation, mines and granaries.

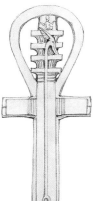

*The pharaoh is often shown holding this symbol. It means 'life'. No one but he can pass the death sentence, or remove it.*

*You are quite likely to see the pharaoh for he travels widely to attend ceremonies and keep an eye on important work. Everyone has a right to appeal to him for justice, though officials will want to fob you off if you try.*

**(Below)** *the rulers of a conquered land have to send yearly gifts to the pharaoh, who is their overlord.*

*These gifts have come from the south – ebony, ivory, leopard skins and heavy rings of solid gold from the mines of Nubia. There is also something new for the pharaoh's menagerie.*

*An official who has pleased the pharaoh may be ceremonially showered with gold gifts — necklaces and cups.*

**SOME MINISTERS**

*Your chances of becoming a minister are remote unless your father happens to be a courtier or a high official.*

*From the left: the Overseer of the Treasury; the Head of Irrigation; the Controller of the State Granaries.*

*This is the Chief Steward. He directs the work of the vast staff of the royal palaces and kitchens.*

*The Director of Building Works who controls craftsmen, mines and quarries; the Commander of the Army.*

*The Governor of a nome, or region. He is a local head of government. Next to him, the Keeper of State Records.*

*A King's Friend, meaning a favoured courtier. Some have titles, like Royal Sandal Carrier or Fan Bearer.*

*You have to put up with the tax men. They measure your crops, or check your work, and note what you must pay.*

The pharaoh's subjects obediently built him temples to offer to the gods, and a majestic tomb to make him live for ever, because they believed that it was he who made the gods favour Egypt. Without their god-king the flood would not come and the people of Egypt would perish.

However, nobody regarded the thousands of officials who carried out the pharaoh's orders as gods. These officials made ordinary people work hard in ways they did not like, and took away many of the people's goods as taxes to be stored for government use.

The most important official was the pharaoh's chief minister, or vizier. He kept his eye on every department of government, and ran the law courts. The ancient Egyptians believed that every person had a right to be given justice.

*The vizier is sentencing some high officials who have stolen goods paid to them as taxes. The courtroom is crowded with other people waiting to put their cases. A just vizier will hear each in turn, regardless of importance.*

*A market official catches a thief. The baboon acts as "sniffer dog" and helps the arrest. Local police keep law and order in the towns, but you may well be set upon by robbers if you travel alone unarmed in the country.*

*When officials order you to dig the canals, you could try coughing and seeming very ill, but this seldom works.*

*There is a way to make life easier. A bribe can make a tax inspector or law court officer much more friendly and helpful.*

*If you cannot prove your case in court you can appeal to a local god, when its statue is paraded through town. (In later years it was kept in court.) You could call out your problem to it – "Lord, who stole my ox?" or, "Who has moved my boundary stones," for instance. The statue may nod at the thief's door.*

*Beating is the commonest punishment. Slaves, servants and hard up taxpayers are beaten as much as their punishers like, but if a court orders you to be beaten the weapon and the number of blows will be stated.*

*Ordinary people act as judges in village courts. A woman is claiming that a policeman has not paid her for a jar of fat.*

## A VIZIER'S DAY

*His early morning is spent reading reports and dictating letters.*

*Other officials report to him. The treasurer gives him an account of the taxes in the store houses.*

*Next he sets off swiftly for the palace to inform the pharaoh of the progress of work in all departments.*

*He spends the rest of the morning judging a legal case – three people's claims to inherit one piece of land.*

*In the afternoon he attends a ceremony to mark the appointment of a Chief Secretary. The vizier hands him his seal.*

*Then he finds he has to go to a court where tomb robbers are being held. He must question them before nightfall.*

## Q

You've been told to bring food to your grandparents' ka. Why do you have to do this?
*Go to page 14*

# WOMEN IN SOCIETY
## WHAT RIGHTS WOULD YOU HAVE?

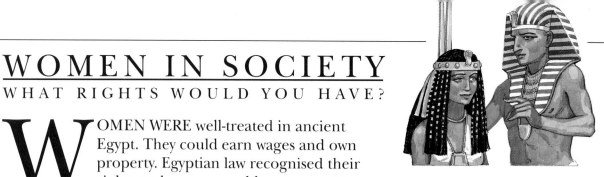

*Signing a contract. As a married women or a widow you can do what you like with your own property.*

*You can inherit separately from your husband. If a will seems unfair to you, you can challenge it in the courts.*

**W**OMEN WERE well-treated in ancient Egypt. They could earn wages and own property. Egyptian law recognised their rights and women could go to court to claim them if they felt they were being treated unjustly. Husbands were expected to let their wives go wherever they wished and do what they wanted.

Women in poorer families had to work, either in the home or the fields or helping in their husband's trades. They made many things which could be used in bartering, so they added a great deal to the family income. Wealthier women prided themselves on not having to work. The role of a priestess was regarded as an honour rather than a job.

From a modern point of view women did not have the same rights as men. Many were well-educated but they were not trained as scribes so almost all careers were closed to them. A woman could become pharaoh, but this was extremely unusual.

*If you are the eldest princess you have a special importance. You, not your brothers, inherit and pass on the sun god's divine nature. Anyone wishing to seize power must marry you, to establish his right to rule. You may have to marry your brother.*

*Queen Ahhotep took power and defeated rebels who killed her husband. She was awarded this ceremonial axe.*

SPHINX- portrait of a famous pharaoh, Queen Hatshepsut. She wears the false beard which is one of the signs of a pharaoh. When her husband died she ruled in his place, because the next pharaoh was too young. She would not give up power when he grew older, and ruled until her death.

*If your marriage ends in divorce you can take your own property and children away with you, and can marry again.*

*In your will you can choose who is to receive your personal property. It does not have to go to your family.*

*Women grind the corn. There must be a quicker way of doing this, but no one has bothered to think of one.*

*Women often took over the running of large estates while their husbands were away in the city.*

*Gleaning is a job peasant women do at harvest time. They gather up everything useful that the reapers have let fall, ears of corn and even single grains, so that nothing is wasted.*

**Q**

You are moving into a new house. Where will you keep all of your possessions? Go to page 17

**YOUR LIFE AS A PEASANT**

*Up at dawn, you boil grain to feed the family.*

*The men must reap the crops. You trudge to town with eggs and home-made mats to sell.*

*When market is over, you clean, grind, bake and join your neighbours to spin.*

*At noon, under the hot sun, you will take the resting men fresh bread to eat.*

*You stay to glean but get into a fight when another gleaner spills your basket and claims your gleanings.*

*You get supper ready and shut up the animals. There is still time for basket-making.*

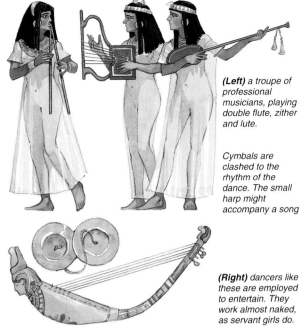

(Left) a troupe of professional musicians, playing a double flute, zither and lute.

Cymbals are clashed to the rhythm of the dance. The small harp might accompany a song.

(Right) dancers like these are employed to entertain. They work almost naked, as servant girls do.

These priestesses hold a type of rattle, called a sistrum, which they shake as they perform songs and dances in the temple, or follow the god's image through the streets.

ABOUT WOMEN

This sistrum has a handle in the form of the head of Hathor, the goddess of love, music and dancing.

Drawing of a girl making up. Lip tint comes from iron oxide, green and black for eyes from copper and lead ores.

If you were to ask an ancient Egyptian why women were not treated equally you would receive a very puzzled look. The idea that people ought to be equal did not enter into the ancient Egyptians' way of thinking. They believed that their world was arranged according to the good example they had been given when the world was new and the gods had ruled on earth. If people treated each other with the respect they deserved everyone's life would be harmonious and happy. Men and women expected to enjoy life together.

If your husband is very rich you may have to share the women's quarters with one or two lesser wives.

A group of professional mourners. They wear robes of blue, the colour of mourning.

Perfume makers shown in a stone relief. In the hot climate it is refreshing to rub one's body with scented oil. They are wringing out a bag crammed with flower petals, so that the precious essence will scent a large jar of oil.

MOURNERS SOB loudly, wail, and rub ashes on their heads, as signs of grief. This is their job. They are not really sad. A grand funeral is not complete without them, for they let everyone know that the death is mourned.

Women, too, may be ceremonially honoured by the pharaoh and showered with gifts of gold.

### YOUR LIFE AS A PRIESTESS

You wake in cool linen sheets and call for your maid to dress you.

When your make-up is finished your children come in to say good morning to you.

Your servants make the townspeople give way as you are carried to the temple.

There is a rota of duties. This month you dance in the stately temple chorus.

Finally the day is free. It is pleasant to join your husband and friends on the river.

Friends will help you to pass the evening, or you can play senet with your husband.

Q

If you were a craftsman, would you be able to work for the pharaoh?
*Go to page 29*

# THE GODS
## WHAT WOULD YOU BELIEVE IN?

The sunset sky is red with the blood of the serpent of evil, who tries to destroy the sun. Horus fights him.

Osiris, **(left)**, lord of the underworld. With him are his wife and sister, Isis, and his evil brother, Seth.

Re, the sun god crosses the sky in a boat which Nut swallows at night. At dawn he is re-born from her body.

Gods often enter a creature sacred to them. You might see Nekhbet, goddess of Upper Egypt, as a vulture.

Though you may not enter the temple you can put offerings of food and wine for the god on tables in the forecourt.

In the beginning, some say, the infant sun god was born from a lotus bud.

The statuettes above show the ibis **(left)** which is a shape taken by Thoth, god of wisdom and writing. The mongoose **(right)** is sacred to Re. He became one in order to fight the evil serpent.

THE ANCIENT EGYPTIANS had many gods. If a region became important, perhaps because a pharaoh had moved his capital there, its god became famous. Re, the sun god, was always worshipped, but in New Kingdom times Amun, the wind god of Thebes, became powerful. Like mortals, each god had a 'ka' which had to be fed to keep its owner alive in the world beyond the grave. The god's temple housed its 'ka' and the offerings brought there were its food.

HOW DID THE WORLD BEGIN?
People's beliefs varied according to where they lived. They tended to think their local god had a hand in it. Most agreed it began as water, from which a mound arose with the life force upon it. This force created the gods. The drawing above left shows the moment when the air god lifted up his newly created daughter, the sky, to separate her from her brother, the earth.

If you need to ask a god for help, have your prayer carved on a tablet of stone and place it on a temple offering table. Put ears on it to make sure the god will listen.

**(Below)** the 'ka' of the god lives in the innermost part of the temple, which priests enter with torches.

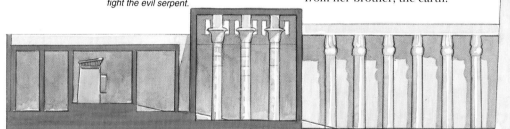

Ordinary people felt that these great gods were unlikely to help with everyday problems, so they made offerings at home to friendly gods like Tauert and Bes. The best loved of all the gods was Osiris, who had died and returned to life. He gave everyone hope of life after death.

# Q

What sort of foods would you eat as an ancient Egyptian?
*Go to page 18*

Jealous Seth slew his brother Osiris and scattered the pieces of his body throughout Egypt. Isis searched for them.

Horus, son of Isis and Osiris, tried to avenge his father who returned to life as king of the underworld.

Osiris figures which have been sown with grain, are put in tombs. The sprouting corn symbolises life after death.

At home you put offerings of food on a stand like this, which represents Bes the dwarf, a kindly and protective god.

On the festival of the cat, goddess Bastet was worshipped at Bubastis, and lion hunting was forbidden.

Gods can have many roles and emblems. Thoth is God of Scribes and also of the moon. The baboon is sacred to him.

# ENTERTAINMENT

## HOW COULD YOU KEEP YOURSELF AMUSED?

**P**EOPLE HAD TO work hard in ancient Egypt, but could also expect to enjoy themselves. They seized every opportunity to have a good time. The festivals of the gods were holidays that sometimes lasted several days, with much singing, dancing, and noise in the streets, and lots of eating and drinking. Indoor entertainments were a luxury for the rich but everyone could enjoy the open air. Hunting and wrestling were favourite sports.

Balls made of painted clay. They are filled with beads and rattle when you throw them.

The best games are simple games that you can play anywhere, like tug of war or ball games.

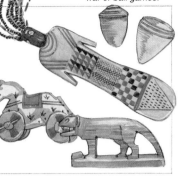

If you have a dog it probably looks like this greyhound type – whether it is a sheep dog, hunting dog or idle pet.

A toy made of carved ivory. When you give the strings a pull the men twirl round and round.

There may be a stall at the market selling wooden dolls with bead hair like this one, and animals that open their mouths, like this cat. Simple toys like spinning tops can be made at home.

When Herodotus was in Egypt he was told people shaved off their eyebrows to mourn the death of a cat. Maybe he was being teased.

*(Above)* a box for playing senet. Two people can play. The top of the box is the board; the drawer holds the pieces. Dice are thrown to decide the moves.

The game on the left is a contest between jackals and dogs. Pegs representing them are moved on the board.

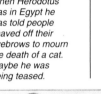

A wealthy family may have a monkey as an amusing pet. Keeping it under control is a job for the servants.

*(Below)* hunting. If you are wealthy enough not to have to catch your own food, you will find this a most enjoyable way of filling the time.

What do you laugh at? Jokes implying that your masters are up to no good!

A lion playing the game of senet with its prey, the antelope.

A jackal acting as a kindly goat-herd and a cat which cares for birds.

*(Left)* hunting in the marshes. A bird flutters up from the reeds. The hunter hurls a throwstick to stun it.

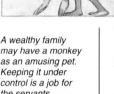

The goose is not a household pet, but some people let it wander into houses because it is sacred to the wind god, Amun.

*(Right)* hunting in the desert. Servants carry back the booty – antelope, gazelle and desert hare.

What do you look forward to? Without doubt it is the festival of the local god which is the great event of the year for everyone.

Priests act plays showing the god's deeds. The huge procession with singers, dancers and music, fills the streets.

The town is packed with entertainers, food stalls and souvenir sellers. Families cook the best feast they can afford.

**Q**

If you were a peasant how many rooms would you have in your house? *Go to page 17*

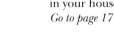

# SICKNESS AND HEALTH
## WHAT WOULD HAPPEN IF YOU FELL ILL?

### DOCTOR, CAN YOU HELP?

*You may suffer from incurable breathing problems. Sand inhaled during sandstorms builds up in the lungs.*

*Coughing can be a sign of parasitic worms in your lungs. A longer sort ends up in your legs. Try winding the worm out.*

*Doctors say many ills are due to people's insides getting out of place. They put the people over hot fumes to draw them back.*

*Eye diseases and blindness are common. Life is hard for the blind, though some find work as musicians.*

### Q

You've decided to join the army. Is this a good career move?

*Go to page 31*

IF YOU FELL ILL in ancient Egypt your chances of getting better were quite high. Doctors kept careful records and knew what methods had worked well in the past. They understood the importance of diet in illnesses and were skilful at setting broken bones. Many doctors were specialists, treating women's diseases, or the eyes, or stomach.

These skills treated only the symptoms of disease. Doctors believed, very sensibly, that they should deal with the causes as well. To the ancient Egyptians' way of thinking all misfortunes without an obvious external cause were sent by evil spirits. It was therefore quite logical for doctors to recite spells over their patients. They also recommended magic potions, amulets and prayers to the gods.

PREVENTATIVE medicine. Amulets give protection against the evil spirits that cause disease. The one above represents the eye of Horus, a sign which is particularly powerful.

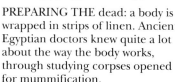

PREPARING THE dead: a body is wrapped in strips of linen. Ancient Egyptian doctors knew quite a lot about the way the body works, through studying corpses opened for mummification.

*(Right)* when the doctor comes he may bring his instruments in a case like this, made of cane and papyrus.

(LEFT) STATUE OF a woman healer with a plaque showing Horus in the form of a child. Prayers and offerings to temple statues like these may help if you feel ill.

*(Below right)* a doctor treats a very sick man. Herbal brews, made with beer, cow's milk or castor oil, are tried.

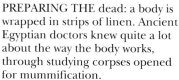

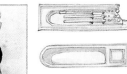

*(Above)* treating an eye that is infected, or inflamed by sand. Stonemasons' eyes often get damaged by chips of stone.

*(Above)* this is a surviving ancient Egyptian instrument case and its lid. A corner is missing.

*Some temples have accommodation for the very sick who are hoping for a miraculous cure. They pray and receive treatment from the priests.*

*Many temple medical schools specialise in women's diseases. At Sais in the Delta the priestesses of the goddess Neith teach midwifery.*

*A pregnancy test. Pour your urine over two bags – wheat and barley. If they sprout you are pregnant. Wheat sprouting first means a girl, barley a boy.*

# SUPERSTITIONS
## WHAT WOULD YOU BE AFRAID OF?

EGYPT WAS A prosperous land with few powerful enemies. The Mittanians and the Hittites (in modern Syria and Palestine) were sometimes hostile but the Egyptians were confident that their pharaoh would always overcome foreign rivals. People were more anxious about the threat of danger from the gods. Seth, the cruel red god of the desert, was the cause of most troubles. There was also the chance that normally well-disposed gods might be offended if they felt themselves neglected. Then the flood would be low, and people would starve.

Death was not something to be feared but it caused a lot of anxiety. Unless you took the right precautions your spirit would not live to enjoy the happiness of the next world. It was essential to have a tomb on which your name could always be read, and to arrange in your will for employees to feed your 'ka' forever.

A foreign captive. The Egyptians do not fear their neighbours. The pharaoh always wins his battles. At least, if he does not, his defeats are not reported.

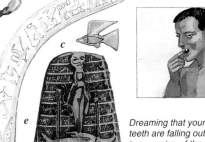

*a b c d e*

To keep you safe: **a.** the god Bes who guards families; **b.** ivory blade with magic signs; **c.** fish lucky charm; **d.** container for a written spell; **e.** protective statue.

A carving showing starving people. In front, one of the causes of famine – the dreaded locust, an insect that flies in great swarms and gobbles up crops.

If you have a warning dream get up at once and recite a prayer to Isis while eating bread and green herbs. This will prevent the dream from having its evil effect.

### INTERPRETING DREAMS

People believe that dreams have meanings. If you dream someone gives you white bread you will be lucky.

Dreaming that your teeth are falling out is a warning of the death of someone very dear to you.

To dream that you have the face of a leopard is a very good omen. You will become an important leader.

If you dream that you are steering a boat you will not succeed in a case you are bringing in a lawcourt.

**(Above)** creatures to beware: snakes (the bite of the asp is deadly); scorpions (from the spider family but with a harder shell) which have dangerous stings; hippos -- they attack when cross; crocodiles who will eat you if they can.

The thirteenth day of the second part of the season of sowing is unlucky because it is the day of Sekhmet, the goddess who sends plagues and diseases. The birthday of Seth, at the end of the harvest, is a very dangerous day. There are many more, some not very good, some more unlucky and some really bad.

**(Below)** a vengeful person is removing someone's name from an inscription tablet. Its owner's soul will die if there is no name for it to be remembered by.

**(Above)** a dreadful fate – death in a foreign land. If you die abroad you will be buried by foreigners, who know nothing about the funeral preparations and ceremonies which guarantee life in the next world.

### UNLUCKY DAYS

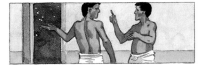

Be careful what you do on unlucky days. It is safer not to go out of doors after dark. On very evil days it is best not to leave your house at all.

Various things become unsafe on different days – bathing, making a journey, lighting a fire indoors, and so on. There are calendars which list what is unsafe and when.

Take offerings to the temples to please the gods. They are more likely to protect you if you do. Do not forget to give offerings of thanksgiving if the gods help you.

Q
If you wanted to make a boat with very little money, how could you do this?
*Go to page 25*

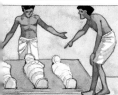

The embalmer shows your family wooden models of various styles of mummy — cheap, mid-range and luxury treatments.

Your family cannot afford the best so your body is just injected with cedar oil, so that its insides will liquify and drain out.

It is then packed round with natron (a type of soda) and left for about forty days. The natron stops it rotting and dries it.

Then the family collect your body for burial. It is very shrivelled but it will not decay because it is completely dry.

Q

If you had a house in the country, what would it be like?
Go to page 17

# MUMMIFICATION
## WHAT WOULD HAPPEN TO YOUR BODY?

If you are prosperous you will build yourself a tomb with an enclosed courtyard at ground level.

Top of the shaft opening into the courtyard.

Burial chamber

THE ANCIENT EGYPTIANS took a lot of trouble getting ready for life in the next world. Everyone who could afford to do so made elaborate preparations. Your spirit had to have nourishment in order to live, and it had to return to your body to receive food. Therefore three things were essential; a body that would never decay, a resting place where it would never be disturbed, and people who would always bring food. Ordering a tomb, built of stone to last for ever, was the first step. All wealthy people did this long before they expected to die. They might also arrange the details of their own mummification, to make sure they were given the best. If they had no family, and were wealthy, land would be left to provide a livelihood for servants who then would feed their ka.

DESIGNING A TOMB. You must make sure that every detail is right. Here a client discusses the wall paintings. A grid of squares has been marked on the wall to make it easy to enlarge the design, which an assistant is showing him for comparison.

(Above) underground burial shaft and tomb chamber, cut in the rock. People enter the shaft from the courtyard and climb steep steps to the chamber. The mummy case is lowered down.

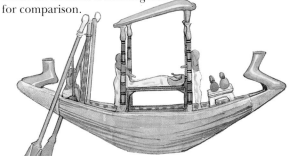

A PHARAOH would have needed a boat in the afterlife in order to travel through the sky with the sun. This is a model of a burial boat.

When the ceremonies were over, your tomb was sealed and funeral guests held a feast in your honour. Meanwhile your spirit rowed over a river to the land of the dead. You had many perils to face on the way, including the weighing of your heart, by which your life was judged. If you followed the instructions in the Book of Magic which was in the bindings of your mummy, all would be well. It contained a spell to recite which insured that your heart would weigh no more than the feather of truth, and you would reach the fields of happiness.

### MAKING THE MUMMY

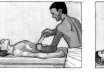

To make you into a top quality mummy your body is cut open and the insides removed.

The brain is drawn out through the nose. Liver, intestines, stomach and lungs are each stored in a special jar.

Your heart is left inside your body which is then put in natron for 100 days. This will dry it out.

Every effort is made to get a life-like look. Parts that become sunken are packed out with linen wads.

Your body is wrapped in layers of linen. Amulets are bound in, to protect you on your journey to the next world.

A face mask of compressed paper, painted to look like you, is put on the finished mummy.

In order to have a comfortable life in the next world you had to take with you all the things you'd enjoyed in this one – food, clothes, furniture and servants. You would have pictures of the life you hoped to enjoy painted on the walls of your tomb.

The pharaohs, who lived in great luxury in this world, needed to fill their tombs with very costly objects for the next. This posed a security problem, for unscrupulous people tried to steal them. The pyramids of earlier times were designed to protect the pharaohs' tombs for ever.

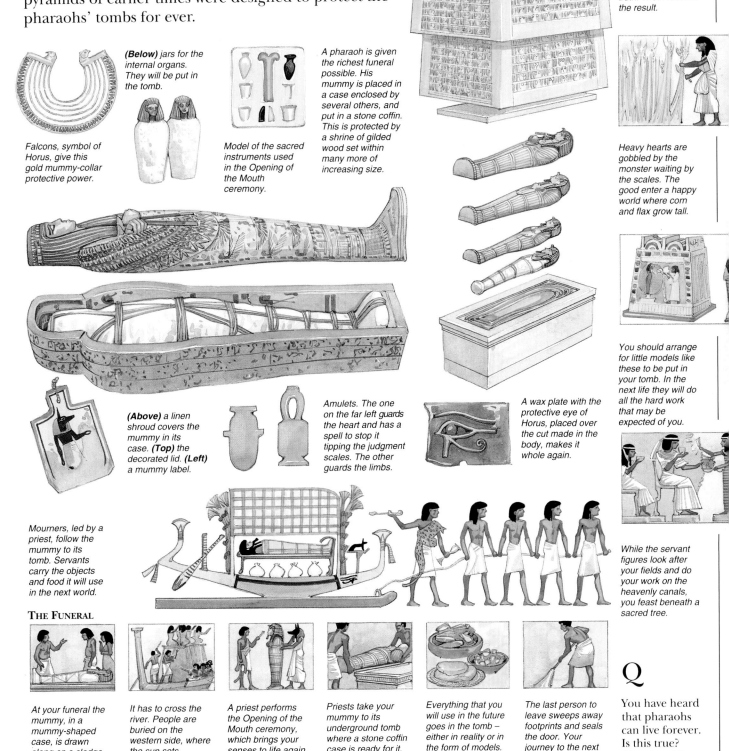

*Anubis, God of the Dead, weighs your heart. Its sins must not outweigh the feather of truth. Thoth records the result.*

*Falcons, symbol of Horus, give this gold mummy-collar protective power.*

*(Below) jars for the internal organs. They will be put in the tomb.*

*Model of the sacred instruments used in the Opening of the Mouth ceremony.*

*A pharaoh is given the richest funeral possible. His mummy is placed in a case enclosed by several others, and put in a stone coffin. This is protected by a shrine of gilded wood set within many more of increasing size.*

*Heavy hearts are gobbled by the monster waiting by the scales. The good enter a happy world where corn and flax grow tall.*

*(Above) a linen shroud covers the mummy in its case. (Top) the decorated lid. (Left) a mummy label.*

*Amulets. The one on the far left guards the heart and has a spell to stop it tipping the judgment scales. The other guards the limbs.*

*A wax plate with the protective eye of Horus, placed over the cut made in the body, makes it whole again.*

*You should arrange for little models like these to be put in your tomb. In the next life they will do all the hard work that may be expected of you.*

*Mourners, led by a priest, follow the mummy to its tomb. Servants carry the objects and food it will use in the next world.*

*While the servant figures look after your fields and do your work on the heavenly canals, you feast beneath a sacred tree.*

## THE FUNERAL

*At your funeral the mummy, in a mummy-shaped case, is drawn along on a sledge.*

*It has to cross the river. People are buried on the western side, where the sun sets.*

*A priest performs the Opening of the Mouth ceremony, which brings your senses to life again.*

*Priests take your mummy to its underground tomb where a stone coffin case is ready for it.*

*Everything that you will use in the future goes in the tomb – either in reality or in the form of models.*

*The last person to leave sweeps away footprints and seals the door. Your journey to the next world has begun.*

Q

You have heard that pharaohs can live forever. Is this true? *Go to page 32*

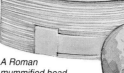

A Roman mummified head, c.AD 300, and a box for ground up mummy. For many centuries European doctors used this as medicine.

Herodotus, an ancient Greek historian, wrote a vivid account of life in Egypt, which he visited in about 480 BC.

THE ROMANS, WHO TOOK over Egypt in 30 BC, had no interest in Egyptian ways and did not even try to understand their hieroglyphs. After the Christians closed the last Egyptian temples in the 6th century AD there was no one left who could read them. The only remaining clues to the history of Egypt were the biblical story of Joseph, the reports of Herodotus, and an account written in the 3rd century BC by a priest called Manetho. He had listed the order and length of the pharaohs' reigns and a few of their deeds. His account is not accurate but it has helped modern scholars to piece together the events of ancient Egyptian history.

One of the many travellers who wondered at the pyramids was the Englishman, George Sandys, who wrote an account of his visit in 1610.

Royal mummies found in secret tombs at Deir el Bahri. The mummies were rediscovered in the late 19th century and taken to Cairo.

In 1769 Piranesi, an Italian artist, published designs in an "Egyptian" style like this strange fireplace.

# HOW DO WE KNOW?

The Arabs, who came to Egypt in AD 641, believed its monuments held magic secrets. This led to the long-held notion of Egypt as a land of sorcery.

Bold travellers went to Egypt, but Europeans knew very little until books about its antiquities were printed. From about 1780 newly designed objects sometimes had an "Egyptian" flavour. This trend became fashionable after Napoleon invaded Egypt in 1798 and had its old monuments recorded.

Napoleon's officers supervise the measuring of a statue. His forces were in Egypt from 1798 to 1801. They included 167 scholars sent to gather information on Egypt. Their research appeared from 1809-13 in twenty four illustrated volumes.

Before the days of proper archaeology adventurers, like the Italian Giovanni Belzoni, stripped tombs to sell the contents. He exhibited his spoils in London in 1821.

In 1799 one of Napoleon's soldiers in Egypt dug up this fragment, now called the Rosetta Stone. On it are three bands of writing, in ancient Greek, in hieroglyphs, and in a late Egyptian script. When scholars realised that the bands were translations of the same text they began to be able to understand the hieroglyphs by comparing them with the Greek.

*Jean François Champollion*

**(Right)** comparing names written in Greek on the stone with the same names written in hieroglyphs proved that hieroglyphs can stand for sounds, as letters do. Previously people had thought they were just symbols.

PTOLMIIS

KLIOPADRA

By 1822 the Frenchman Champollion had deciphered the Rosetta Stone, making it possible to read inscriptions and to understand ancient Egyptian life. Nineteenth century archaeologists went to dig for evidence. Among the greatest were the Frenchman Mariette, who started true excavations instead of random looting, and the Englishman Flinders Petrie whose systematic methods established the science of Egyptology. By studying the remains of temples, tombs, objects, inscriptions and wall-paintings, reading fragments of papyrus and sifting the sand for evidence, Egyptologists have recovered a lost world.

The little sphinx-heads decorating this 1860 set of Italian jewellery show that the "Egyptian" craze continued.

Colossal statues outside the temple at Abu Simbel.

On the brink of the most sensational find of all – Howard Carter about to unseal the tomb of Tutankhamun in 1922.

The keen traveller Amelia Edwards sketching at Abu Simbel in 1874. She wrote about her journey in "1000 miles up the Nile".

**(Left)** X-Raying a mummy in the neuro-radiological department of a hospital. X-Ray pictures help in deciding sex and age at death. They show where amulets are placed and if there are substitutes for missing limbs. They may reveal disease and even the cause of death.

The teeth of this mummy are visibly worn down, probably because bread was coarse and full of grit.

Cameras are used to explore sites. Here a camera is lowered from scaffolding to probe what proved to be a burial boat.

A computer model of the Great Sphinx at Giza, made by feeding in all available information. Reconstructions of lost parts were added to the computer image. The image can be viewed from any angle.

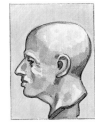

Reconstructing a mummy's features from its skull. A flexible mould of the skull is made, in two halves.

The halves are cast in plaster and joined. The face is built up on this foundation by adding plaster.

Scientists know what thickness of flesh is likely to be found at twenty-six fixed points on a human skull.

Using this information the correct amounts of plaster are added at those points and a portrait emerges.

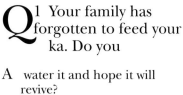

# HAVE YOU SURVIVED?

**Q1** Your family has forgotten to feed your ka. Do you

A  water it and hope it will revive?
B  get another from the cattle market?
C  face total death?

**Q2** A nome is

A  the period of time it takes to make a mummy?
B  the area ruled by a regional governor?
C  a little statue placed in a tomb, to do work for the dead in the afterlife?

**Q3** If you were the Royal Sandal Carrier would you work

A  only in the dry season?
B  only in the flood season?
C  only symbolically?

**Q4** Natron is used for

A  building a house?
B  for mummification?
C  for cooking fish?

**Q5** Senet provides

A  a way of passing the time?
B  a red dye?
C  a substitute for sugar?

**Q6** What did the ancient Egyptians make in a mould and bake in the sun?

A  papyrus?
B  bread?
C  bricks?

**Q7** You want to take your ancient Egyptian family a small present from the modern world. Which would be the best surprise?

A  some writing paper?
B  a bunch of bananas?
C  some home made cakes?

**Q8** If you were a priest which one of these would you certainly not wear

A  a woollen wig?
B  a leopard skin?
C  make-up?

**Q9** The papyrus plant can be made into paper, but also you can

A  make it into sails?
B  weave its fibres into linen?
C  eat it?

**Q10** Women howl and beat their heads

A  as a sign that they are divorced?
B  to ward off evil spirits?
C  to show grief when someone dies?

**Q11** A shaduf is

A  a vizier's assistant?
B  a device for lifting water?
C  a type of loaf sweetened with honey?

**Q12** Pilgrims journey to Abydos to honour the well-loved god

A  Horus?
B  Osiris?
C  Tauert?

**Q13** The Rosetta Stone enabled scholars to read hieroglyphs, because its ancient Egyptian text was repeated in a language they knew, which was

A  Greek?
B  Latin?
C  Hebrew?

**Q14** If you were speaking of the god Horus which of these remarks would an ancient Egyptian disagree with?

A  his symbol is the falcon?
B  he is the son of Osiris?
C  he is the son of Re, the sun god?

To find out if you have survived as an ancient Egyptian check the answers on page 48.

THE KINGDOM OF ANCIENT
Egypt lasted for over three
thousand years – more than one-
and-a-half times as long as the time
that separates us from the ancient
Romans! To make this huge stretch
of time easier to grasp, historians
describe it as three long periods of
prosperity, with shorter spells of
civil war and invasion in between.
They call the long periods the Old,
Middle and New Kingdoms
('kingdom' in this sense means a
period of time, not a realm) and
the breaks they call Intermediate
Periods. They group the pharaohs
in dynasties. A dynasty is a
succession of rulers belonging to
related families.

The Nile valley was settled in
prehistoric times by peoples from
surrounding regions who came
looking for more fertile land. At
first chieftains ruled small areas.
These in time came to form two
kingdoms - Lower Egypt (the Delta)
and Upper Egypt (the south).
Egypt's recorded history begins in
about 3100 BC when, according to
an old story, the two kingdoms
were united by a great warrior
called Menes. He became the first
pharaoh of all Egypt and built a
capital at Memphis.

2686-2181 BC is the time of the
Old Kingdom when Egypt is ruled
by the third to the sixth dynasties of
pharaohs. It is a peaceful period.
Huge stone pyramids are built, to
provide the pharaohs with
everlasting tombs. The most
famous are the three at Giza –
the Great Pyramid, built c.2566 BC
for Cheops, a pharaoh of the fourth
dynasty, and the pyramids of his
son Chephren and of Chephren's
successor Mycerinus which stand
nearby. The Great Sphinx, an
enormous man-headed lion at the
approach to Cephren's pyramid,
dates from this time too.

2181-2133 BC, the First
Intermediate Period. The authority
of the pharaohs weakens. Local
princes seize the chance to take
control. They fight each other to
gain power.

2133-1786 BC, the Middle
Kingdom – eleventh to thirteenth
dynasties. A prince from the city of
Thebes reunites the land and a
second great age begins. Trade
increases, huge marshes are
drained, splendid tombs and
temples are built and a chain of
fortresses is made to keep out
envious invaders from the east.

1786-1567 BC, the Second
Intermediate Period. Asiatic
invaders, called the Hyksos,
conquer Lower Egypt. They bring
horse-drawn chariots to Egypt.

1567-1085 BC, New Kingdom –
eighteenth to twentieth dynasties.
The Egyptians of Upper Egypt drive
out the Hyksos and reunite the
country. The pharaohs begin
overseas conquests, eastwards in
Syria and Palestine, and
southwards in Nubia.

Egypt grows enormously rich,
trading in African gold and
controlling the mines of Asia. The
temples at modern Karnak and
Luxor (Thebes) and the great
temples cut into the rock at Abu
Simbel (in Nubia) are built. The
Egyptians have to fight wars with
hostile rival powers, especially with
the Hittite people of what is now
Turkey. Under later, weaker rulers
Egypt is attacked by one enemy
after another.

728 BC An army from the
south puts Nubian pharaohs on
the throne.

661 BC The Assyrians capture
Memphis and Thebes.

525 BC The Persians become
masters of Egypt. The Egyptians
hated them most of all.

332 BC Alexander the Great drives
out the Persians and puts Greek
pharaohs on the throne.

30 BC Egypt becomes a province
of the Roman Empire. The old
beliefs are forgotten. Temples and
palaces fall into ruins and are
buried by the sand.

# GLOSSARY

ADZE tool with the blade at right angles to the handle, for chipping wood.

AMULET a small object, either worn or carried, which was thought to ward off evil.

ANVIL a support for hammering metal into shape.

AWL a tool for piercing holes.

BARTER to buy or sell something by exchanging it for objects of equal value.

BELLOWS a leather bag squeezed to produce a strong blast of air.

BOW-DRILL a drill encircled by the string of a small bow. When the bow was pushed backwards and forwards the string made the drill rotate.

BRANDING making a permanent mark on the skin with a piece of hot iron.

BRAZIER a small container in which a fire is made.

CHASE to decorate metal by punching or raising its surface with a tool.

CRUCIBLE a pottery container in which metal is melted.

DELTA a fan-shaped area of small rivers and land formed where a large river divides to enter the sea.

DYKE an artificial channel of water, sometimes between high banks.

EGYPTOLOGIST a scholar specialising in the study of ancient Egyptian history.

EMBALM to preserve a dead body by treating it with scented oils and spices.

FAIENCE a glass-like substance made from powdered quartz used in making jewellery and ornamental tiles.

FERMENT to produce alcohol by the action of natural sugars and yeasts in a liquid.

GAUGE a marked scale, on a wall or stick, etc. against which objects can be measured, by comparison.

GAUZE a very thin transparent fabric.

GESSO a mixture of ground up chalk and glue which is applied to wood. When dry it provides a very smooth surface which can be painted, or covered in gold leaf.

GLEANER a person who gathers up ears of corn left by the reapers.

GOLD LEAF gold which has been beaten as thin, or thinner, than a leaf.

GRANARY a building in which grain is stored.

GRANITE a very hard rock.

GRILL an open-work pattern of metal or brick covering a window or opening.

HARPOONING using a harpoon - a lance-like weapon thrown to spear fish or other water creatures.

IBIS a bird related to the heron.

IBEX a wild goat, found in mountainous areas of Europe, northern Africa and Asia.

INFANTRY soldiers who fight on foot.

INGOT a lump of metal, cast in a mould into a shape and size suitable for handling.

LIMESTONE a light-coloured, easily cut rock, much used for building.

MATTOCK a digging tool, with the blade at right angles to the handle.

MORTAR a cup-shaped container in which food or other substances are pounded.

MIDWIFERY the science of helping women in childbirth.

MONGOOSE a small agile animal. Various types live in southern Europe, Africa and Asia. They eat small mammals, reptiles and eggs.

MORTISE a small hole cut in the surface of a piece of wood to receive the projecting end of another piece, so as to form a joint.

NATRON a form of soda, found in the ground in some parts of the world.

PLUMBLINE a length of thread with a stone or lead weight at one end. When allowed to hang freely it provides a true vertical line.

QUAY an artificial landing place built for the unloading of boats.

QUARTZ a very common hard mineral, found as rock and in sand. It occurs in many colours, or is transparent. Some rarer forms are semi-precious.

REAPER a person who cuts corn.

RITUAL used in a religious ceremony.

SCARAB a type of beetle.

SEAL a small object with a design cut into its surface. When pressed into melted wax it leaves an impression of the design upon it. Documents were marked in this way to prove their ownership.

SHEAVES bound up bundles of newly cut corn.

SHIFT a woman's long straight undergarment.

SHRINE a cupboard-like container in which the image of a god is kept.

SHROUD a cloth in which a body is wrapped for burial.

SYMBOL an object, or drawn shape, which stands for something else. Symbols often represent ideas, such as 'life' or 'love', which cannot be shown in any other way because they are invisible.

THONG a narrow strip of leather, used as a lace or strap.

VENEER a very thin layer of wood which is fixed to the surface of an object made of cheaper wood, to give a decorative finish.

WINNOWING using the air to blow away unwanted bits of grain-husk.

# INDEX

ACKNOWLEDGEMENTS
The Salariya Book Co Ltd would like to thank the following people for their assistance:

Sarah Ridley
Penny Clarke

## ANSWERS

### HAVE YOU SURVIVED?

Here are the quiz answers, with pages to turn to if you need an explanation.

**Q**
1 (C) - page 14
2 (B) - page 32
3 (C) - page 32
4 (B) - page 26
5 (A) - page 37
6 (C) - page 16
7 (B) - page 19
8 (A) - page 21
9 (C) - page 14
10 (C) - page 35
11 (B) - page 27
12 (B) - page 24
13 (A) - page 43
14 (None) - pages 32, 46 & 41

Count up your correct answers and find out what your survival rating is.

13 - 14   Excellent! You would be rewarded by the pharaoh.
10 - 12   You would make a capable scribe.
6 - 9     Best to pay your taxes, and stay out of trouble.
5 - 0     Terrible! You are likely to get a beating.

PRINTED IN BELGIUM BY
proost
INTERNATIONAL BOOK PRODUCTION